LOVE:

Decoded

CENTENNIAL BOOKS

LOVE: Decoded

Pamela Weintraub

CENTENNIAL BOOKS

CONTENTS

~

CHAPTER 1
FALLING IN LOVE

10 How Love Conquered Marriage
20 Finding "The One"
28 Science of the Happiest Marriages

CHAPTER 2
MAKING IT WORK

40 The Marriage Road Map
54 The Arcs of Love
66 Marriage Makes You Healthier
78 Married With Children
86 The Good Fight
90 Complex Relations
96 Feathering the Empty Nest

CHAPTER 3
PERFECTING THE UNION

106 Spice It Up
118 The Art of the Orgasm
126 Why We Smooch
128 Doing It Right
138 Words of Love

Decoding Love

THE STRONGEST AND MOST POSITIVE EMOTION CAN DEEPEN AND GROW WITH EACH PASSING YEAR.

Romantic love has long been celebrated, yet in the context of marriage, it was a second thought, at best. Instead, marriage of the past was a practical affair: People wed for financial security, to create family, to have a home. Today the most enduring unions enable love, a life well-lived and the chance for personal growth. This book celebrates the 21st-century reinvention of love and marriage, with input from experts at the forefront of the field. Stephanie Coontz, who wrote the seminal social history of marriage, explains how love has emerged as a driving force. David Schnarch, who reinvented sex therapy for a new generation interested in deep connection, describes his model for relationships where partners can be independent while sharing their lives. And Aaron Ben-Ze'ev, preeminent philosopher of love and author of *The Arc of Love*, explains how long-term relationships can enable personal growth. It's not all about flights of passion and soulmates: We also cover the gamut of pragmatic issues, from finding "the one" to getting along with the in-laws, collaborating on parenting and refeathering the nest when the kids have gone. Plus, you'll find advice from couples married for 50 years or more. ("Dance," one woman told us. "Keep talking," a man said.) In the new vision of love, these acts draw us out, deepen our connections and endure.

CHAPTER 1

Falling in Love

THE INTENSITY AND CONNECTION
IN THE EARLY DAYS OF A
RELATIONSHIP SET THE STAGE
FOR A LIFETIME OF COMMITMENT.

ANTONY
AND
CLEOPATRA

Richard Burton and
Elizabeth Taylor's real-life
passion was evident in the
1963 film *Cleopatra*.

How Love Conquered Marriage

THEY WERE ONCE BUSINESS ARRANGEMENTS
MEANT TO PROTECT OR GROW PERSONAL WEALTH.
NOW, MATRIMONY IS ALL ABOUT CARING,
PASSION, EMPATHY AND LOVE.

The story of marriage was not always a tale of love. For thousands of years in human history, marriage was a financial enterprise meant to solidify power and consolidate money, land and labor—and not just for royalty but for the poor as well. Then things changed. In the interview that follows, author and historian Stephanie Coontz describes how, over the course of a few hundred years, the institution gradually morphed into the pursuit of mutual happiness. Coontz also relates why the "love" story of Antony and Cleopatra makes her laugh—and offers the secret to a satisfying modern marriage. (Hint: It involves sharing responsibilities.) She is the author of the seminal book on marriage history, *Marriage, a History: From Obedience to Intimacy, or How Love Conquered Marriage.*

Q **What is the greatest change that marriage has undergone in the past few centuries, and what was behind it?**

Until the 1970s, the greatest change in marriage over the previous four centuries was the gradual acceptance that individuals should freely choose their own marriage partner on the basis of love. For thousands of years, marriage was not about love. It was the way that the ruling classes made military alliances, signed peace treaties and

"Only rarely in history has love been seen as the main reason for getting married."

–Marriage, a History

bolstered their claims to royal descent. For the lower classes, it was the most important decision they would make for their livelihood, since family farms and businesses required the labor of both men and women. Love was gravy— nice if it came along but not essential.

Many young people used to dream of being able to combine love and marriage, but it was only during the 17th and 18th centuries that this became both possible and socially acceptable. The spread of wage labor meant that a young man didn't have to wait until his parents died to inherit a farm or business, so he could afford to set up his own family, with or without their permission. A young woman could earn her own dowry by working as a servant or textile maker.

Q Can you describe the rise of the love match?

The new ideal of the love match spread rapidly in Western Europe and America, but has taken longer elsewhere. Not until this century, for example, did Saudi Arabia pass a law saying a man couldn't force his daughter into marriage. And arranged marriages are still common in many countries, though children have more input and veto power than they used to. But to understand the dilemmas and opportunities facing modern couples, it's important to remember that the ideal of the love match rested on a very different definition of love from what we're now trying to put into practice. Love was seen as a union of opposites, uniting a man, who specialized in one set of skills and emotions, and a woman, who specialized in another—with little overlap.

Q What is your favorite example of a marriage from the past that contradicts our modern beliefs about tradition?

I always laugh when I hear Antony and Cleopatra lauded as a great love story. They may have had good sex, but mostly it was a ruthless scheme to gain immense political power. Egypt and Rome were the greatest empires of the ancient world, and what a coup it would have been to unite and rule them both. Cleopatra

LANCELOT AND GUINEVERE

In an expression of courtly love, Lancelot kneels before Guinevere (in a 19th-century engraving based on the 12th-century original).

displayed her ambitions early, by going to war against her co-ruler brother to be sole pharaoh. In Rome, Julius Caesar was still the dominant political leader. So when Caesar came on a diplomatic mission to end the war, both he and

Cleopatra were delighted when their bedroom diplomacy resulted in a child. They went back to their lives, but he now had a son, Caesarion, with a claim to rule Egypt, and she had a son with a claim on Rome.

After Caesar died, Cleopatra then seduced Antony, who was one of the three claimants to Caesar's title—and you can bet he was infatuated by both her political and erotic assets. He remained married to Octavia, who had important political connections in Rome, for some time. But at a certain point in the struggle for power, he divorced Octavia and joined with Cleopatra, and together they fought for the right to rule Rome "on behalf" of Caesar's young son. When they lost, they killed themselves, well-aware that if they'd been taken back to Rome, their deaths would have been much more painful.

Q How does our idea of "traditional" marriage differ from marriages past?

The idea that a "traditional" marriage is one man, one woman, monogamous, and based on true love may be many people's ideal today, but it's not how marriage used to work. There have been many types of marriage over the millennia, and perhaps the single most approved one— mentioned most often in the first five books of the Old Testament—was one man, many women.

NAPOLEON AND JOSEPHINE

They married in 1796, and he crowned her empress in 1804. He divorced her after he concluded she could not conceive a child, but her name was the last word on his deathbed.

"By the end of the 1700s, personal choice of partners had replaced arranged marriage as a social idea."

–Marriage, a History

~

PRINCE GRIGORY AND CATHERINE THE GREAT

The dashing prince and the Russian tsarina were lovers for years, but stayed close friends even after their passion waned.

Q Even after monogamy became the legal norm, it was often not the actual practice. Can you explain?

For centuries, men felt free to have affairs outside marriage, and women just had to put up with it. We have letters of men bragging to their friends and even in-laws about affairs they had, and from fathers telling their daughters that it was unseemly to complain about a husband's behavior. Today, disapproval of marital infidelity is probably at an all-time high. But the flip side is that people are more accepting of premarital sex and less judgmental when people choose consensually to organize their sex lives in a different way. It's also important to remember that the male-breadwinner family was the least traditional— and most short-lived—marriage form in history.

Q What lesson can modern couples take away from what history has to tell us about marriage?

Well, kindness, patience and a willingness to negotiate have always made marriages better, while contempt or abuse has always made them

MILLENNIAL WATCH

Those born after 1980 are reinventing marriage
in their own image: It's often done later in life; is more diverse;
and is far more fluid in style, pace and celebration.

⇥ TAKING THEIR TIME

Millennials are getting married at a slower and lower rate than previous generations; they also lag in leaving parents' homes and having kids. About 44 percent of millennials between ages 25 and 34 were married in 2015, compared to 68 percent of baby boomers during a similar period of life. The lag is not only due to a desire for more education and more women working, but also the Great Recession of 2008 and student loans. Millennials got such a late career start that average marriage ages for men and women are now 30.9 and 29.2, compared to 22 and 20 in the 1950s.

⇥ MIXING IT UP

The most important thing about the millennial generation is its diversity—44 percent are minorities and 14 percent (about one in seven) have interracial marriages. This is almost three times the rate (5 percent) seen in boomer marriages that came before.

⇥ BABIES BEFORE MARRIAGE

Millennials are more likely to have children before marriage. A record 55 percent of parents aged 28 to 34 have put childbearing before marriage—more than double the share of boomers at the same age. The trend may increase hardships for members of this group. "Young adults who put marriage before any childbearing are much more likely to avoid poverty and find themselves at least in the middle class," note social scientists from the Institute for Family Studies, who did the research.

⇥ FLEXIBLE ROLES

Millennials are far more likely than previous generations to blur gender roles in areas from moneymaking to child care to housework. Millennials are also far more accepting of gay marriage, with 74 percent approving of same-sex marriage, compared to just 56 percent of baby boomers.

worse. But today, perhaps the most important thing we can learn from history is that history doesn't offer us a lot of guidance for modern marriages. It is only during the past 40 years that we have begun to build our marriages on the basis of males' and females' similarities instead of their differences.

Q The average age of marriage has risen, and most wives have as much education and job experience as—if not more than—their husbands do. How are we dealing with that? Marriage requires more negotiation and friendship than when it was the man who was more educated, more experienced and the primary breadwinner. Most men and women expect equality and sharing today, not specialization and male leadership. As a result, all the rules for having successful relationships are changing.

Q What are some keys to marital success? One of the strongest predictors of both marital and sexual satisfaction today is sharing housework, child care and breadwinning, rather than having each partner specialize in one job. Researchers say that men are actually most happy when they share the responsibility for shopping with their partner, and women are the most unhappy when their partner does not share responsibility for the dishes.

PARTNER UP– BUT SKIP THE WEDDING

IN SOME SOCIETIES, when people form a lifetime partnership, they're increasingly forgoing formal marriage rites. In the U.S., marriage rates among older people are outpacing those of younger couples: In 2016, 55.3 percent of people aged 65 or older were married, whereas 48.6 percent of adults under age 64 were—a record low, according to the U.S. Census Bureau. Young Europeans also aren't feeling very pro-marriage. Wedding rates in France and Spain have bottomed to historic lows. Only a handful of European countries, including Germany, are holding steady on the marriage front.

THE REASONS for the declines vary but include general apathy toward marriage as an institution and economic considerations that preclude having a costly celebration when current social attitudes allow young people to simply live together. In the U.S., less education and lower income are associated with not marrying.

GERTRUDE STEIN AND ALICE B. TOKLAS

They fell in love the day they met and were partners for the next 39 years (seen here, circa 1940).

Finding "The One"

THE KEY ELEMENTS WILL SURPRISE YOU.

lga Zemskova was crushed when her husband died suddenly due to a hospital error. Their long marriage "felt like one beautiful day," she says. "We just laughed and laughed for 18 years. And then it was nighttime—and he was gone."

Fleeing reminders of her lost love, she left her home in Odessa, a seaside city in Ukraine, and came to the United States. Again fearing reminders, she chose her current husband, in part, because his personality is so different, she said. They, too, have been happy together for 18 years.

Her story illustrates an important message about love: You can be happy with different people, not just one "soul mate," and your ideal mates may not even fall into one personality type.

The idea that we each have a single fated match dates back to the ancient Greek philosopher Plato as well as the Jewish Talmud. Modern psychologists like Arthur Aron, who has studied romantic love for decades, say the notion leads us astray. "Don't stress out about meeting 'the One,'" he says.

"Chemistry," unlike a soul mate, isn't a myth. But it's not all that important. Even similar tastes weren't the key to Zemskova's success. So what is? Not wanting to specify the differences between two husbands, Zemskova simply says, beaming, "They're both sweet."

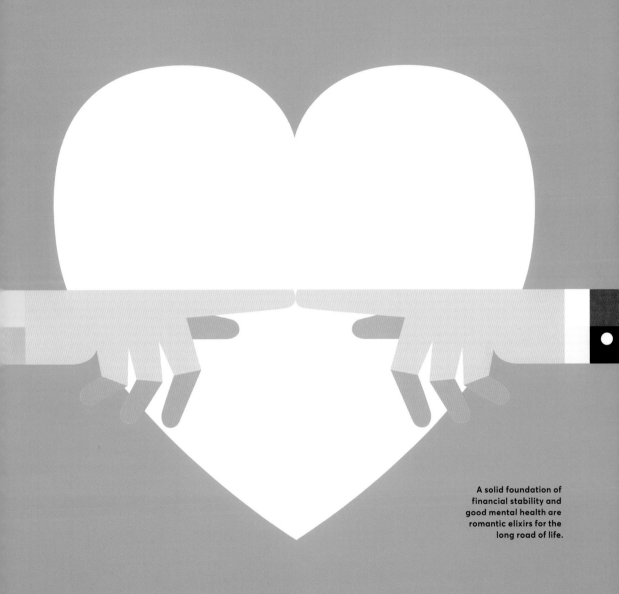

A solid foundation of
financial stability and
good mental health are
romantic elixirs for the
long road of life.

⚜ Chemistry Is Real

Online dating profiles, of course, refer much more often to "chemistry" than sweetness. Our bodies do have strong preferences: A person's scent reveals telltale clues about a group of genes called the major histocompatibility complex (MHC), which influences tissue rejection. If a woman conceives with a partner whose MHC is too much like hers, her womb is more likely to reject the fetus. A potential lover's scent with dissimilar MHC may trigger immediate lust. In one of many studies of this theory, women preferred the T-shirts of men whose MHC was dissimilar to their own; they said the smells reminded them of their current or former mates. (But if they were taking birth control pills, they liked MHC-similar men). Saliva carries similar clues, suggesting that the first kiss is indeed a big test.

That spark of love is caused by three neurochemicals: norepinephrine, dopamine and phenylethylamine.

~

You'll sometimes hear the argument that powerful chemistry keeps people together during the hard times. One couple, who met after each had divorced, considered it so central that they inscribed "I love your sniff" in their wedding rings. "Even during our worst times, if we breathe each other in, we reconnect," the woman explained. "Since we both work at home, I sometimes have to be careful to keep a little physical distance, because if we smell each other, we might end up in bed." Seven years into the relationship, they were still making love 10 times a week.

But even when chemistry leads to early intense romantic feelings, it's not a guarantee of success, nor is it necessary. "Those who are intensely in love in the beginning are slightly more likely to have a good relationship—but only slightly," says Aron. "Talk to anyone in India, and they will tell you that people can fall in love later on. It's a romantic ideal there."

A better test might be how you feel emotionally after sex. Most people are conscious of feeling an afterglow for about a half hour. Emotions about your partner may actually linger for up to 48 hours, according to a 2017 study that concluded that couples who experienced stronger afterglows were happier in their relationships six months later. And emotional closeness—yes, sweetness—can feed passionate sex, even over years, other research suggests.

Look for a partner who can support your biggest dreams and celebrate your wins.

✤ Birds of a Feather

Daters who are less focused on sex at the beginning of a relationship may seek someone who is easy to get along with, at least at first, because they're similar. "The more similar two people are, the more likely they are to form a stable, lasting relationship and be happy," says social psychologist Viren Swami, the author of *Attraction Explained: The Science of How We Form Relationships.*

In practice, we choose partners with roughly the same levels of education, IQ, family wealth and looks. We even favor mates with similar genes for height and weight, according to a 2017 study of nearly 25,000 couples. The pattern shows up among other animals as well: An Eastern bluebird with especially bright feathers will find another bird that is brighter than the pack, for instance, and big Japanese common toads spurn smaller ones.

FINDING LOVE ONLINE

Two-thirds of Americans believe in soul mates, according to a 2017 survey of 800 adults. A good first step in making your love match through a dating app, however, is to abandon that fantasy, which can make people ditch promising relationships over trifles.

Here's how to get the most out of your online experience.

DON'T UNLOAD Avoid self-sabotage by posting morose photos and confessing serious problems on first dates. Depression, addiction and bad finances won't get you far.

WOMEN, MAKE THE FIRST MOVE OkCupid reports that 30 percent of first messages sent out by a straight woman to a man turn into a conversation, compared to only 12 percent of first messages sent by straight men. Also, research shows men tend to reach out to women who they feel are more attractive than they are.

POSE WITH A PET For women, the profile photos most likely to lead to conversations are those in which they're doing something; next are photos with an animal. Men get more messages from women when they look in the distance in their photo or pose with a pet. **FILL OUT THE BIO** Men with blank bios are 98 percent less likely to get a match.

TAKE PERSONALITY PROFILES WITH A GRAIN OF SALT Neither sex should invest much time examining personality profiles and online answers to questions. Most people can't judge from profiles who they'll like in person.

BE AUTHENTIC Specify the pragmatic characteristics you actually want—and stick to them. If you dream of a family with a Jewish woman, skip the hot Catholic actress.

LET IT GO Feeling ghosted? Demanding explanations, obsessing or tracking your date's activities won't help. It's an easy trap: As *New York Times'* "Modern Love" editor Daniel Jones observes, "nearly everyone cyberstalks." But it's best to just move on.

DECIDE IF YOU'RE A GOOD BET Get therapy, if needed, and make it your business to change for the better.

Couples are now more likely to meet a partner online than through friends.

gravitated together because you're both Southerners living up North with MBAs, but one of you is careful and solitary and the other impulsive and sociable. It doesn't matter. In fact, a meta-analysis of more than 300 studies found that similar personality measures had zero effect on couple satisfaction. Chris Portman, a psychologist in Bellingham, Washington, who works with couples, says, "We used to give people a compatibility scale and say, 'You'll never make it because you two are too different in important areas like religion, politics and sex.' Then the real research came out."

Scientific efforts to pin down ideal pairings that boost harmony also haven't panned out. Now Portman advises couples that all duos have conflict—troubles and disagreements that can't be completely resolved. Happy couples, he says, keep humor and affection flowing, making small gestures or jokes even in the midst of battle.

Over time, communication counts more than your early connection. "The happy couple's happiness can deteriorate quickly, while people who may start off less happy will get happier if the couple practices good skills," Aron says.

✚ Red Flags

Clinical psychologists John and Julie Gottman have identified four kinds of behavior that predict divorce: criticism, contempt, defensiveness and

✚ Love Is Blind

Don't worry, however, if you think your partner's looks put him slightly out of your league. Love is indeed a little blind: It's common to mistakenly think your partner is better-looking than you are, Swami and others have found. Your partner, ideally, thinks he got lucky. That belief isn't a sign of low self-esteem on either side: According to Swami, confident, extroverted people are *even more* likely to think they have landed a catch.

Like chemistry, similarity in taste or personality isn't essential. Let's say you stonewalling. Given the findings, you may want to screen potential dates with these common dating-site scenarios in mind:

When you're angry at your partner, you might take a break and stop talking with or seeing each other for...
A A day or two.
B Up to two weeks or a month.
C No more than an hour.
D Permanently. Some things you just can't talk out.
Answer The best here are A and C.

In a fight, it's OK to...
A Make a joke here and there—but not at the other person's expense.
B Curse and insult the other person.
C Slam doors and throw things.
D Analyze the other's psychology, rolling your eyes.
E Repeat criticism voiced by your friends and mother.
Answer The only good response here would be A. On the other hand, if both of you can laugh about your differences, that may be the best sign of all.

Find a Booster

Supporting each other's dreams is another good sign. Yvonne and Roger Puckett are a wonderful

Research shows that intense attraction and infatuation tend to last about three to four months into a relationship.

example: After he saw her dance in a show aptly named *The Boyfriend*, he came backstage and "followed me around," she says. "One day, it hit me—we were going to be friends." They built a friendship over three years before getting married, exactly 50 years ago. Their large dance community came to celebrate their golden anniversary.

Much as we'd like to make the search for love into a science, scientific answers sound a lot like common sense. When a couple shares similar criteria like education and family wealth, they generally have a better chance for success than when these factors differ too much. When these elements match, good mental health and financial stability make you a catch. Choose someone who is healthy and whole. Find a partner who will support your biggest dreams and celebrate your successes. And fight kindly. It's well worth it.

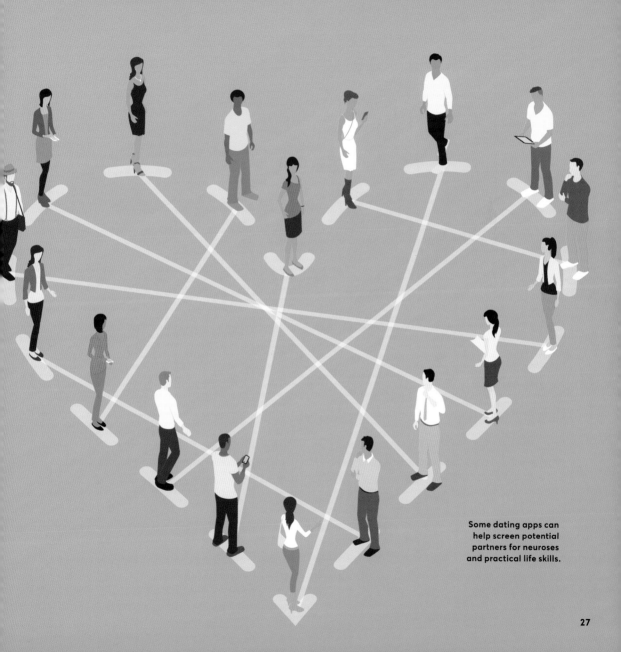

Some dating apps can
help screen potential
partners for neuroses
and practical life skills.

Science of the Happiest Marriages

THE MOST ENDURING PARTNERSHIPS ARE BUILT ON EMPATHY, TOLERANCE, JOY AND RESPECT. SECRETS OF THE LONGEST UNIONS ARE REVEALED HERE.

Burk and Sophia Villee of Pittsburgh say that their relationship was strengthened by a major difficulty they experienced early in their marriage, when their young son fell ill. "When our son, Charlie, was 2 years old, we found out that he was sick," says Sophia. "He had special needs, and he died when he was 25. We decided that we were going to have to make our marriage work, and that kept both of us working very hard to stay together.

"Losing our son was so hard. Nobody can ever tell you what that's like," Sophia adds. "But we're the best of friends now. We rely on each other. If we ever have a disagreement, we don't argue. We just enjoy each other's company, and we are so

Complacency is the biggest indicator of difficulty in a long-term relationship.

Falling in Love

Being emotionally responsive to your partner's needs will keep you close.

grateful for everything we do have. And if there's something we don't have, it's just not that important. We have each other."

Today, with some 50 percent of marriages ending in divorce, the unions that thrive for 25 years—let alone a half-century or more— must be unique. How do these couples flourish in each other's presence, nurturing each other and growing as individuals year after year?

The question has piqued the interest of social scientists, who have been studying this elite group of long-distance runners for insight into their success. In one marriage, the husband and wife disagree on everything from politics to religion, but they seem strong and happy as a couple. In another, the couple seems to check all the boxes of compatibility, but the two spouses

feel distant after years of growing apart. Researchers are now finding what makes the difference so stark: When couples have frequent positive interactions, including conversations in which each partner can express their own needs and receive empathy, the marriages tend to be happier and last longer. When these elements are missing, marriages fall apart.

◆ Remember to Air Your Differences

One recent study published in *Anthropologist* by a group of Turkish researchers found that marriages that last at least 25 years are characterized by good communication— in which both partners express love and respect for one another. In addition, that

---

50+ YEARS OF ADVICE

DON'T STAY ANGRY
"Ten minutes after an argument, we're discussing the menu for dinner. We may disagree, but we never take it seriously."
—*Charlotte*

COUNT YOUR BLESSINGS
"The smartest decision I ever made was asking the right person to marry me. It was the most important thing I

ever did. I married the smartest woman in the world." —*Norton*

● *Charlotte and Norton Feldstein, San Francisco; married 67 years*

---

communication is received with high levels of comprehension, understanding and empathy.

Somewhat counterintuitively, study participants reported that in order to keep their marriages happy, they would actively choose to enter *into* conflict rather than avoid it. But this wasn't about trying to start a fight. On the contrary: These husbands and wives wanted to know their partner's opinions, even if they were vastly different from their own, so that they could discuss them and come to an agreement.

The key here is that empathetic spouses want their partners to be happy. They want each other to feel heard and taken care of. The goal is to win as a couple, rather than chalk up individual wins.

Psychologist Gülen Uygarer of Eastern Mediterranean University, the study's lead author, says that compatibility between partners is subjective and impossible to measure—but empathy is always essential to any marriage. "Who cannot be a compatible partner?" asks Uygarer. "A liar? A racist? Someone who is disrespectful, jealous or selfish? I cannot define a compatible partner in general. I can only list what sort of characteristics I would like my own partner to have.... I also cannot tell you if empathy or choosing a compatible partner is more important, because choosing a compatible partner is related to personal interests. However, empathy is essential to any happy and successful interpersonal relationship," including marriage.

Other studies have had similar findings. According to a 2017 study, couples who have frequent positive interactions, including

50+ YEARS OF ADVICE

FOCUS ON CHARACTER
"Choose a partner who's fundamentally good—and seek real evidence for that. How do they treat you? Does the person accept that you have your own life and ideas and not try to change them?" —*Linda*

TAKE RESPONSIBILITY FOR YOUR HAPPINESS
"In the tough times, try going to counseling instead of a lawyer. Learn to deal with your own baggage." —*Denny*

● *Linda and Denny Smith, Dayton, Ohio; married 50 years*

In a committed relationship, both partners must have the ability to make decisions and act.

supportive communication in which they accepted each partner's point of view, tend to stay married longer. These successful couples also tend to share a "couple's identity," in which they think of themselves as one unit who maintains shared values. Even if they have certain values and beliefs that differ from their partner's, they tend to primarily focus on the ones that they share. These characteristics help partners to think of each other in a positive light, to want each other to be happy, to forgive each other after fights.

✤ Pay Attention to Your Partner's Softer Side

Why is empathy so important to marital happiness? The answer seems simple enough: People want to feel heard and to have their opinions valued. They want to matter. As the foundation for most family units, marriage would seem to be the most likely avenue to fulfill that need, so it's only natural that spouses would want empathy from each other.

Psychologist Stephanie Weiland Knarr, a relationship expert and therapist working in metropolitan Washington, D.C., agrees. As part of that empathy, she notes, communing with your partner's softer emotions can be an essential key.

Couples who understand each other's sadness, disappointment and fear are better able to work through problems and differences. When a person knows from experience that they will likely receive empathy from their spouse for their underlying worries and anxieties, they are far more likely to express their needs, which enhances the overall quality of the relationship. "Suppressing needs and feelings, on the other hand, creates a sense of helplessness that can lead to anxiety and depression," Weiland Knarr notes.

✤ Provide Your Partner With 'Customer Service'

To avoid this outcome, both partners must remember to communicate their darker, softer emotions and the needs that those feelings stir up. Then each partner must strive to respect those needs and meet them the best they can.

"I encourage people to know that they are valuable; when they bring up their needs or make complaints in their marriage, that is a good thing!" Weiland Knarr emphasizes. "Especially when they understand that their partner values them."

In fact, Weiland Knarr suggests that we each think of ourselves as running a customer-service counter for our marriage. When our partner brings up an issue, we should provide validation, and then ask how we can best resolve our partner's complaint.

"Often, needs are expressed in the form of one partner bringing up a complaint—such as, 'When you came home late without calling, it really made me feel unimportant and scared. I need for you to call me and let me know when you are going to be getting home later than planned,'" she notes.

"Research shows that in a healthy marriage, needs are expressed in this softer way—called a soft startup—not in a harsh way, like yelling or

Go with the flow and try not to sweat the small stuff.

50+
YEARS
OF
ADVICE

GIVE SOME SPACE

"There are days when we get really upset with each other. But it never lasts. We have our time alone...and then whatever it is that's bothering us is over."
—*Mary Ann*

LET IT GROW

"I used to think of marriage like a rope and in rocky times strands would get cut, so the rope would weaken. But it's the opposite: You start with one strand, and as your marriage grows, more fibers are added."
—*Peter*

● *Mary Ann and Peter LaPorte, Leonardtown, Maryland; married 51 years*

---

through expressions of anger," adds Weiland Knarr. "If a partner then responds with defensiveness, like, 'Stop nagging me, it's not a big deal,' that reaction is a predictor of marital dissatisfaction and divorce. Ideally, a partner will accept responsibility for their mistakes and agree to solutions that will meet their partner's needs. This is a predictor of success."

When operating your customer-service department, the best currency is empathy itself. Every marriage has disagreements. It's hard to imagine that any married person has never felt hurt or insulted by their spouse. But in a happy marriage with a good level of empathy, each partner is able to express their feelings about those hurts in a constructive way. And more

importantly, their partner listens and tries their best to solve the problem.

✦ Have a Sense of Humor and Try to Let the Little Things Go

Peter and Mary Ann LaPorte of Leonardtown, Maryland, have been married for 51 years. They agree that it's important to listen to your partner's complaints with empathy, but it's equally important to not let those problems bother you.

According to Mary Ann, the keys to a happy marriage are a combination of patience and humor. "I think I have been blessed with the gift of patience. Everybody tells me that, and I believe it," she says. "So I try not to let little quirks bother me. We all want things done certain ways, myself included. And sometimes you can go with the flow, and other times you'll bump heads. I try to reduce the number of times that we bump heads, to make it smooth —and certain things I just try to ignore."

✦ Don't Keep Score— Play as a Team

Peter agrees, and adds that couples should think of themselves as a unit that wins together, rather than individuals with competing needs and goals: "I see a lot of couples that keep score. You know, who spent what, and so forth. That's inevitable, I think, from time to time, because it's just human nature to say, 'I get that, and you get this.' But I think a happier marriage is not a scoreboard. You recognize that you might be behind in one inning but not the other, and you just let it go. It's not something by which you live your life or you say, 'Well, that's yours, and this is mine.' It's ours. It retains that sense of community, if you will."

The science concurs. "The secret behind the survival of a long-term marriage and continued satisfaction within a marriage is, generally, effective communication skills," Uygarer concludes. "Respect, patience, tolerance, understanding, caring for each other and listening" are the secret ingredients. These help the partners achieve harmony, and they serve as complements to that all-important factor—love.

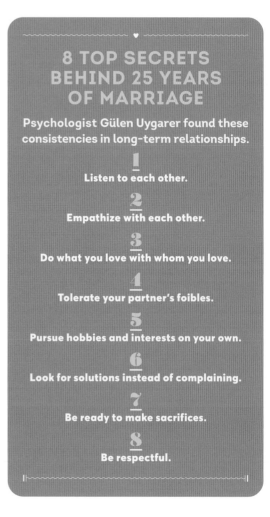

8 TOP SECRETS BEHIND 25 YEARS OF MARRIAGE

Psychologist Gülen Uygarer found these consistencies in long-term relationships.

1
Listen to each other.

2
Empathize with each other.

3
Do what you love with whom you love.

4
Tolerate your partner's foibles.

5
Pursue hobbies and interests on your own.

6
Look for solutions instead of complaining.

7
Be ready to make sacrifices.

8
Be respectful.

Pull together when setting a course for your life. Remember, you are teammates, not competitors.

CHAPTER 2

Making It Work

YOUR LONG-TERM UNION
IS A SYSTEM: LEARN HOW TO
NAVIGATE YOUR JOB, KIDS AND
YOUR IN-LAWS TO KEEP THE
RELATIONSHIP ALIVE
AND FLOURISHING.

The Marriage Road Map

SUCCESSFUL MATRIMONY IS AN INTRICATE PROCESS OF BALANCING AUTONOMY AND CONNECTEDNESS. HERE'S A PLAN FOR THE MOST IMPORTANT RELATIONSHIP SKILLS.

I t's all uphill from Denver to nearby Evergreen in the foothills of the Colorado Rockies. And that's perhaps as it should be. I'm on my way to interview David Schnarch, the New York–born psychologist who has spent decades upending everything we thought we knew about true love, passion and hot sex. Especially hot sex.

Once considered a heretic, Schnarch is today a distinguished presence in psychology, a pioneer set on redefining intimacy and reinvesting marriage with the passion that usually fades. "It's easy to have hot sex with a stranger," Schnarch insists. "But a passionate marriage requires that you become an adult."

And this, he admits, is a challenge. Becoming an adult means going against the whole drift of the culture. It means, among other things, soothing your own bad feelings without the help of another, pursuing your own goals and standing on your own two feet. Most people associate such skills with singlehood. But Schnarch says that marriage can't succeed unless we claim our sense of self in the presence of another. The resulting growth turns right around and fuels the marriage—and the passionate sex. It also pays wide-ranging dividends, from friendship to creativity to work.

Success means
sharing both
the good times
and the bad.

♣ A Radical Idea

To understand just how subversive such thinking is, it helps to know that Schnarch has been articulating his ideas about the emotional and erotic power of independence within relationships just as mainstream psychology has almost unanimously endorsed attachment as the heart of adult relationships. In fact, Schnarch finds that our preoccupation with attachment, with its ideal of feeling and acting as one, keeps partners infantile and overly emotionally dependent—enmeshed, in the language of psychology; "fused" is the way Schnarch puts it.

Applied to infants, attachment theory has value. The consistent attention of a caregiver allows a helpless baby to develop emotional security, the hallmark of which is his growing ability to explore the world on his own. Extended to marriage, attachment implies that if couples can simulate that early bond, they'll bask in emotional security for life.

> ## *Romantic love has more room to grow when it is given space.*
> ~

Schnarch contends that marital attachment often doesn't leave enough space for partners to speak their minds, think their own thoughts or attain their ambitions and dreams. Attachment not only reduces adults to infants but also reduces marriage to a quest for safety, security and compensation for childhood disappointments. "We've eliminated from marriage those things that fuel our essential drives for autonomy and freedom," says Schnarch. "It becomes a trap that actually prevents us from growing up. Instead of infantilizing us, marriage can—and must— become the cradle of adult development."

The path to this goal is differentiation—the dynamic process through which you can live in close proximity to a partner and still maintain a separate sense of self. "By differentiation, I mean not caving in to pressure to conform from a partner who has tremendous emotional significance in your life." The best marital brew is neither dependence nor independence but a balanced state of interdependence, Schnarch contends.

Interdependence allows partners, each of whom is capable of handling their own emotional lives, to focus on meeting both their own and each other's ever-evolving goals and agendas in response to shifting circumstances, rather than on keeping one another from falling apart. It is marked by flexibility and focuses on mutual strengths.

Making eye contact with your partner increases intimacy.

Dependent partners, by contrast, spend their lives compensating for each other's limitations and needs.

It's not that hard to be independent when you're alone, Schnarch observes. But pursuing your own goals and standing up for your own beliefs, your personal likes and dislikes, in the midst of a relationship is a far tougher feat. Once it is achieved in the context of a relationship, differentiation becomes possible outside it as well. If you can stand your ground with your partner, who means so much to you, then you can defend your turf at the office and maintain your principles when pressured.

Claiming adulthood is actually an evolutionary mandate, Schnarch insists: "About 1.2 million years ago, the human cranium evolved to maintain a sense of selfhood. There is lust, there is romantic love, there is attachment. But the strongest desire comes from the self's ability to choose another self." Only the differentiated can truly be known and loved for themselves.

♣ An Eye-Opening Shift to Passionate Love

The path to differentiation runs straight through sex. But not just standard Saturday-night sex.

Schnarch came of professional age as a sex therapist in the 1970s, at the height of the Masters and Johnson era. For William Masters and Virginia Johnson, intimacy was largely a matter of mechanics. The big sex killer was anxiety—the cause of rapid ejaculation, erectile dysfunction and general failure to perform. To rid a couple of anxiety, partners were first to avoid all sexual contact for months. Then they were instructed to focus on the physical sensations of touching each other in turns, giving feedback as to how to make the touching better. Eventually they progressed to intercourse.

Schnarch thought it an adolescent approach, preoccupied with technique and anathema to the deeper emotional connection that heightens responsiveness in adults. As an assistant professor at Louisiana State University in New Orleans, Schnarch was listening to his own patients. Among them were a husband with erectile dysfunction and a wife resistant to

Passionate love intensifies when partners are free to express their thoughts and follow their dreams.

the idea of sex therapy at all. "Don't tell me to do that hokey stuff," said the wife, referring to the then-standard touching exercises. Indeed, great sex is not about technique but about feeling close.

From his clients, Schnarch found that married couples often wished they felt in the bedroom what they felt just making eye contact with strangers walking down the street. Call it sizzle.

Now, that is truly intimate—looking someone in the eye while making love, really seeing them. One couple Schnarch saw, Theresa and Philip, had been married 30 years. They still had sex once a week, but reaching orgasm was difficult. Theresa was plagued by insecurities: She worried about her appearance, and she anticipated rejection—no matter what she did. On the verge of retiring from his job, Philip wondered whether having a new partner would do better at turning him on.

"There was more involved here than lack of passion and feeling inadequate," Schnarch soon realized. After 30 years, Theresa and Philip no longer even kissed during sex. Further, Theresa complained that Philip continually failed to touch her the way she wanted—despite her many explicit instructions on just what to do and how. On the surface, they were lazy during sex. Underneath, Schnarch realized, they were isolated by a fear of getting close.

Schnarch ultimately advised them not to pursue touching in any specific way but to actually feel each other—to follow an emotional connection into sex, not the other way around. Instead of just relaxing to reduce anxiety, they had to tolerate the discomfort of wanting to be wanted—and the potential for rejection that implied.

And they were to have sex with their eyes open, an experience likely to jolt the most closed-off couples to change. "To feel comfortable looking each other in the eye," says Schnarch, "you have to confront conflicts you've swept under the carpet. You aren't likely to let your partner look deep inside you until you've done that yourself."

HOW TO CARRY YOUR OWN WATER

Making your partner responsible for your psychological problems and your past can poison your love.

BE YOUR OWN PERSON Reject the idea that you and your partner must be attached at the hip—always in sync. Sure, you share common moral values, but one can love hiking while the other reads Russian lit.

DON'T TELL YOUR PARTNER HOW TO THINK OR FEEL Allow your partner freedom of speech, feeling and thought. He or she should be able to share their feelings with you—or others—without worrying that you will jump in to argue or replace their inner landscape with your own.

PURSUE YOUR DREAMS AND AMBITIONS Just because you are part of a committed couple does not mean you are barred from having goals of your own. You and your partner must encourage each other to go out into the world and seize the day.

Making It Work

Being able to stand alone keeps you both on equal footing.

Love is more than wild sex and a walk in the park.
~

Eyes-open sex drills right to the heart of differentiation and drives the process of growing up. Closed-eyes partners can get close enough to copulate—but not so close that they have to confront the differences between them or delve into who they actually are. The discomfort of eyes-open sex, on the other hand, heightens connectivity. Physical sensation and emotional connection become integrated rather than remaining separate dimensions that can ultimately interfere with each other. At the same time, the sense of individual selves is enhanced.

♣ Path to Interdependence

Eyes-open sex helped bring couples closer, but because it is also confrontational, it seemed at direct odds with the entire field of marriage therapy, which prescribed compromise and calm as the way to work things through. Then Schnarch discovered the work of Murray Bowen, a pioneering psychiatrist at Georgetown University who was in the process of revamping family therapy. He, too, saw the limitations of attachment theory in relationships.

Classic attachment theorists contend that those with emotional problems received too little love and support from their families. Bowen argued that it didn't necessarily follow that more love and attention would make them whole—in fact, they had become overdependent on love. They needed

END THE MIND GAMES

Your relationship can be destroyed if you and your partner manipulate each other or inflict mutual harm.

REJECT MUTUAL SADISM

Not only are most people aware of the mind games they perpetrate, but they're also aware that their partner is aware that they're aware, a dynamic David Schnarch calls mind-mapping, after the brain's ability to make a mental map of how another mind works.

A man sees an overweight woman on the street and comments disparagingly on her girth to his wife, then insists he didn't realize that his wife, at virtually the same weight, would feel wounded.

The next day, the woman goes on about the success of her old friend the investment banker, despite the fact that her husband has just lost his job. At some level, they both know she is returning the pain.

The insidious nature of such exchanges could be one of the best-kept secrets in marriage: Partners are perpetually involved in collusion, clearing a path of mutual sadism directed pointedly at each other.

One partner or the other may often come to the anxiety-provoking—and disappointing—realization that their partner has been mapping their mind, and not just noting, but *relishing*—their pain. Those who are overwhelmed by that recognition are likely to retreat back into collusion. The road back is clear: It's essential to stop playing mind games and confess any hurtful intent.

UNMASK COLLUSION

One husband was so averse to sex, he hid in the basement whenever the topic came up. Yet when a therapist asked the pair to gaze into each other's eyes, it was the woman who panicked. It turned out that she had chosen a mate whom she knew could not engage emotionally. Her own father had been cruel, and her family never looked one another in the eye. The wife attacked her husband for being disconnected—but on a deep level, he understood that she was no more capable of intimacy than he was.

By confronting each other, the couple were able to talk honestly about their issues and improve the marriage.

to break the dependency while maintaining the closeness—in short, by differentiating from their families of origin and their adult partners, to keep individuality intact. The goal was not to retreat into the security of infancy but to complete the process of growing up.

Indeed, Schnarch now saw, in one clinical session after another, the most troubled couples were often far too enmeshed in the very relationships they complained were not close enough. And they typically felt obligated to seek approval from a partner instead of feeling confident about their own thoughts and actions—the sign of the adult.

One couple had formed their early relationship based on reciprocal emotional disclosures about childhood traumas, old flames and other life events, talking for hours on end. But years into the marriage, the husband shrank from what he considered constant emotional soul-searching. "I don't like being opened up like a fire hydrant," he declared. The more the husband withdrew, the needier the wife became, until divorce loomed. Demanding his empathy and getting none at all, the wife felt rejected and unloved.

Schnarch couldn't help but note the irony: By demanding empathy, this wife was, in essence, seeking approval, or validation, from her husband —a phenomenon Schnarch calls other-validated intimacy. After disclosing her innermost feelings

Learning to handle your own problems can bring you closer together.

only to find rejection, the wife now felt bereft. She began selecting what she revealed more carefully, diminishing not just intimacy in the partnership but her own sense of self.

Forget empathy. Schnarch sees a better approach in self-validated intimacy. "You say what you have to say, and your partner either gives a supportive response or says, 'That is the stupidest thing I ever heard.'" Either way, you pat yourself on the back, respect your own thoughts and feelings and maintain your sense of self-worth. Instead of asking someone for a stamp of approval, you do what any grown-up does: approve of yourself. When you say what you think without fear of rejection, your partner loves and respects you more, because they know who you really are.

And when you become your own person within a relationship, you leave room for someone else to do the same. Instead of depending on a partner to help you manage your own feelings and maintain your equilibrium, you are free to choose to be with your partner. "You can offer your partner a hand instead of just your needs," says Schnarch.

♣ Getting Through Gridlock

Marriage, it turns out, is a system unto itself. And that system has unique, built-in hurdles to happiness. Their purpose is to provide the pressure for people to grow up. Dating is one thing. As Schnarch describes it, "We date, and you see only what I want you to see. I tell you some pseudo deep, dark secret and we feel close and we have sex."

But with marriage, "You may start out talking about all that deep and important stuff, but eventually it gets used up. Then we make deals: I want to spend time with the boys. You want time with your friends. We agree. But now we have used up all the things we agree about, and we are left only with the things we disagree about." Couples become gridlocked. It provokes anxiety. But to Schnarch, therein lies the best chance most people ever get for growing up: a trial-by-fire crucible.

Susan and Mike were budding fiction writers who met at a writers' workshop. Over the two years they dated, they passionately critiqued each other's work and would meet up with other writer

friends to brood over art and childhood traumas. Sex and independent films completed the scene.

Marriage was far less romantic. Working at a dental journal that he felt sapped his soul, Mike railed at Susan when she gained 10 pounds and routinely trashed her writing. When he spent hours playing video games in the basement, Susan called him a "loser jerk."

Schnarch compares marital gridlock to an intricate Chinese puzzle, with each partner's movement blocked by the other's position. At a standstill in their relationship, Mike and Susan began impeding each other's dreams. One wanted a city apartment; the other, a house in the suburbs. One wanted children to follow strict routines; the other wanted freewheeling fun. They would not adapt to each other, nor would they confront their own roles in the standoff.

Gridlock in marriage is absolutely guaranteed. After all the late-night confessionals and wild sex, after all the walks in the park and vacations with

Eyes-open sex is far more rewarding and emotionally close.

~

Developing emotional intelligence can strengthen your bonds.

friends, after the children have gone to bed and the bills have been paid, only gridlock remains.

And there's just one road out of gridlock if you want to keep your marriage intact. You can't communicate your way out of it. You can't empathize your way out of it. You have to learn to soothe your own discomfort, regulate your own emotions, pursue your own goals. Stop being a drain on your partner and handle problems on your own. That way, Schnarch says, you "open enough space" to get closer and make room for passionate love to return.

Gridlock creates anxiety, anger, feelings of rejection and emotional pressure, Schnarch observes. And when these negative feelings become unbearable, the relationship must either change or break apart. Those couples who stay together must look within themselves for insight, confronting their roles in maintaining the conflict.

"The only solution is for one person to differentiate, moving forward and making room for their partner to grow as well," he notes.

Stung and crippled by Mike's critiques of her writing, Susan finally stopped showing it to him. Instead, she sent it to national magazines. They were far more accepting, and Susan met with some success, whether Mike approved or not. Mike converted his desire to structure his children's lives into participation in sports, an

Communication and collaboration will keep you moving in the same direction.

outlet they enjoyed; Susan was largely uninvolved. When Susan worked on a book that was almost derailed because her editor was fired, she solved the problem by finding another publisher without mentioning the crisis to Mike. He developed a set of friends with whom he played tennis weekly.

Yet when the couple decided to take a break, the distance allowed them to reconnect, be flexible in meeting each other's needs and have something to talk about beyond kids and bills.

Equality plays a crucial part in every relationship.

~

✤ Balancing Acts

The elements of maturity, Schnarch has found, can be separated into four distinct, if interrelated, groups that he has named the four points of balance.

One involves operating according to deeply held personal values and goals, even when pressured to abandon them. The second revolves around handling one's own inner emotional life and dealing with anxiety and emotional bruises without needing to turn to a partner for help. A third focuses on not overreacting to—but still facing—difficult people and situations. The fourth point involves forbearance and perseverance in the face of failure and disappointment in order to accomplish one's goals. The four groups emphasize resilience, because they also involve the ability to adapt and change direction when need be, without losing track of one's overall primary love relationship and sense of self.

Adapted from an article published in
Psychology Today

Sure, differentiation is a complex feat, but Schnarch is creating an operational road map. Starting with a list of component skills that were first developed by Bowen—they include withstanding peer pressure, collaborating with others, controlling one's own anxiety, persevering in the face of difficulty and changing direction when further struggle is futile or foolhardy—he has, so far, field-tested the list on more than 4,000 people.

Passionate love
can launch a
lifelong journey.

The Arcs of Love

AARON BEN-ZE'EV, A PROFESSOR OF PHILOSOPHY,
EXPLAINS HOW ROMANCE AND PASSION
CAN SURVIVE IN OUR LONGEST RELATIONSHIPS.

Is love best when it's fresh? Conventional wisdom says the answer is yes. The intensity of new love is impossible to replicate, leading those in long-term relationships to fantasize about something else. But in this Q&A, University of Haifa philosopher Aaron Ben-Ze'ev, known for his insightful writings on the varieties of love, argues that when people can grow and flourish in their long-term relationships, true romantic love can survive, enabling a deep connection far more profound than anything possible when love is new. In his book *The Arc of Love*, Ben-Ze'ev shows how love can become more nourishing as years go by. Here, he shares his insight on what can make love truly last and why the long road is the one best taken.

Q **Is love better when it's new or after steeping and growing for many years?**

It's been said that both eggs and love are best when fresh. Certainly it's true for eggs, in terms of both taste and nutrition. Love also tastes better when fresh: the excitement, the desire. But it's a different story for the nutritious value of love. To get the best out of each other, we must know each other. That takes time.

Q **Let's discuss the beginning— when love is new.**

That's when love is intense. We feel sexual desire, the wish to touch and to be with each other. We are constantly thinking about each other. Frequency of sex decreases considerably over the first years. The arousal from a new partner is always greater than the arousal from a familiar partner. Sexual attraction is greatest when love is fresh. But this is always brief.

An ideal relationship combines both emotional closeness and sexual intimacy.

~

Early intensity in a relationship helps to make an enduring romantic connection that fuels lasting growth.

FLUIDITY: GENDER ID/SHIFTING ROLES DON'T ALTER THE NEED FOR LOVE

In the United States, diversity and flexibility are coins of the realm, especially for millennials and the generations that follow. "People applaud great diversity in food, in their activities," Aaron Ben-Ze'ev says. Demography and culture tell the rest of the tale: Ethnic minorities will comprise more than half the population in the U.S. by the 2040s, promising far more interracial marriages than ever before. And whether we're discussing bathrooms or the sex on a driver's license, the concept of a single, permanent gender has come under increasing scrutiny.

Our gender roles are certainly in flux. Household chores are shared by all. Same-sex marriage is now accepted, and many young people claim a fluid sense of gender regardless of their sex at birth. But despite this revolution, the lust for passion and the need for stability remain competing parts of our deep human nature, Ben-Ze'ev says.

SEEKING VARIETY:
WHEN ONE IS NOT ENOUGH

Those who crave both variety and stability commonly have affairs—in fact, seven in 10 married people claim they've been unfaithful at least once. But Aaron Ben-Ze'ev says that another form of long-term relationship can be seen in about 5 percent of those in the U.S. and the West: polyamory.

Polyamory means loving a few people at the same time, Ben-Ze'ev explains—but rather than being characterized as mere casual sex, it involves stable, intimate relationships within a circle of lovers. Rather than being a deception, it is entirely in the open.

⇉ THREE OR MORE

"One version of polyamory is that in which a group of three or more lovers consider themselves married to each other and allow romantic relationships within the group," Ben-Ze'ev explains. In another version, one person carries on an intimate relationship with more than one partner in different locales. There is consent among the participants, Ben-Ze'ev says.

⇉ LIMITED ENERGY

Like the rest of us, he notes, polyamorists have only so much energy to go around. So, to accommodate that, they "sometimes differentiate relationships as primary, secondary or tertiary in describing the varying levels of commitment involved." Monogamy and exclusivity do not have sole claim over committed relationships: "When polyamorists love each other, they experience and exhibit wholehearted devotion exercised within a restricted environment," Ben-Ze'ev says.

"A person can be devoted to two lovers," he adds, but everyone has a limit to their capacity for love. He quotes relationship researchers David Barash and Judith Lipton: "What makes human beings unusual among mammals is not our penchant for polygamy but the fact that most people practice at least some form of monogamy." Every relationship takes effort, and no one can have an infinite number of loves, no matter what.

Q **The real question is: How can love continue as it matures? How can love stay?**

This is difficult, because emotions are generated by change. When we can feel a significant change in our situation, an intense, acute emotion is generated. But in older love, you must create change internally, by continuing to grow. You have to develop. The intensity is less than with fresh love, but it is in view for a longer time.

Q **Then old love has some advantage?**

Yes. While time is not good for romantic intensity, it is essential for romantic profundity.

Q **What is romantic profundity?**

It is a deep connection between the two partners. They know each other better. They accept each other more totally. And they bring out the best in each other. This is the No. 1 secret for the success of the long-term relationship. This couple will say, "When I am with him or her, I am a better person." What underlies this is what, in psychology, we call the Michelangelo phenomenon. Michelangelo said that when he saw the marble that was in front of him, he could already see the figures in the stone. The dust was gone, and the vision for what he wanted to create was already there.

Physical closeness enhances the emotional connection.

Q **How do we get there?**

It starts early in the relationship, with that intensity to make the connection, so the two will want to be with each other—otherwise, they will not invest the energy and time—and it could be a one-night stand. Love at first sight is very beneficial for beginning the relationship, because there is such great attraction—and that helps make the connection.

After the connection is there, you must keep having a dialogue and you need to do activities together. The activities must have intrinsic value, not just helping with dishes or watching TV but, for instance, hiking in the mountains—something that has personal, inner value and can be shared. These activities should involve just

Long-lasting love isn't just based on physical attraction.

the couple. You have to bring fulfillment to your spouse and yourself, or you will not stay.

Q We've gone from passionate to profound—but what makes this romantic?

It is not the case that profundity is without intensity. It sustains the intensity—but at a more reasonable level. If it remained like it was at the beginning, you would not be able to do other things, because you would be thinking about the beloved all the time. You would not be able to personally flourish. When there is profundity, the attraction is there—it doesn't have to be mainly sexual, but an attraction to be with each other. What is central is the wish to do things together.

Q Yet we have so many distractions and attractions, including old flames, constantly beckoning online.

Today, with so many romantic options, love is in the air. If you have a problem in your relationship, why try to fix it instead of just throwing it away and finding someone else? The problem is that to have profundity you need a lot of time, but we spend less time with each other than ever before. Statistics show that couples spend less time together than they did 20 years ago, and in the time they are together there is less relating. Psychologists have shown that for couples who

> *Quality is as important as quantity when it comes to spending time together as a couple.*
>
> ~

do stay together, the quality of the time spent is very high. In the 1960s in the United States, in addition to practical matters, in addition to love, marriage began to require self-fulfillment. The successful marriage now had demands that even fewer people could meet.

Q So love is not enough?

One woman told me, "I loved my first husband very much and he loved me, but I wasn't flourishing with him. He didn't stop me from doing what I want, but he didn't help me to do it, either." Her second husband she fought with all the time, but he helped her fulfill her dreams.

Q What else do we need for a high-quality union?

Equality, autonomy, reciprocity.

Q Do we need love at all?

If there is great personal flourishing, you may give up your requirement of love. The good-enough partner may not be high on all three scales—the pragmatic, love and flourishing—but is of sufficient quality on each to enable marriage. You don't need the maximum for each, and you can play with the three elements. Love loses intensity with time, but personal flourishing in the marriage lowers the need to put so much weight on love alone. Now you don't have to be madly in love in order to stay married if you are fulfilled—and if the practical matters are working, why leave it?

Q And if you don't meet the minimum thresholds for success in your relationship?

It's much easier and less costly to get out of a marriage than it used to be. And there are a lot of alternatives out there for other partners.

Q Because of the dating apps?

Yes.

Q And if people want to stay in a marriage but also increase their sense of passion?

Romantic love is complex—but open love, in which partners agree to let others in so they can have that intensity, is more complex still. According to statistics, about 20 percent of people have open

For love to be lasting and profound, personal characteristics should be in harmony.

marriages [where they openly have sexual relations with others] and 5 percent live in polyamory [a group "marriage" of three or more.] These relationships are not impossible, but they are very hard. Take a woman with a husband and a lover. Her lover has a wife and her husband has a lover—and her husband's lover has a husband. Now you are talking about six people—at least. The woman now may have greater sexual fulfillment with two partners, the husband and the lover. On the other hand, she has to devote much more time to the relationships for all of them to work out. The intensity is greater, but the length of these

♥

PROFUNDITY:
LIFE IS BEST WHEN YOU LEARN
TO FLOURISH IN LOVE

In this age of the internet, it's harder to settle down and easier to stray. Dating apps give us apparently endless choices for the next new thing. And despite a longtime marriage, old flames and crushes flicker into view from the distant past, offering the kind of high-octane intensity we last experienced when we were 16.

"Computers have changed not just the way we work but the way we love. Falling in and out of love, flirting, cheating, even having sex online have all become part of the modern way of living and loving," says Aaron Ben-Ze'ev, who studied the issue in detail in his book, *Love Online*.

"Our quest for deep, profound kinds of relationships finds itself in crisis, and two reasons stand out: Passionate love, which has such a mighty pull, is by its nature superficial and brief. And in the age of the internet, the potential for these relationships has become great.

"The ideal in committed frameworks is that passionate love is essential for marriage, and that the two spouses create a fused identity," he states. "This has upgraded the value of marriage—but also made marriage more volatile and less certain, since passionate love and marriage do not necessarily go together. When marriage depends exclusively on passionate love, which can change and decrease as time passes, the thought of leaving a marriage" begins to enter each partner's mind.

In our cyber era, says Ben-Ze'ev, "there are many roads available for a romantic journey. People are tempted to pursue superficial romantic experiences rather than investing effort in deepening their current love." Just remember, he warns: More is not always better. Take care when you step online that you don't jeopardize the potential for enduring connection and true flourishing available at home.

relationships is briefer—not just with the second partner, the lover, but with the husband as well.

Q This is why so many have garden-variety affairs?

The majority of couples—about 70 percent of those in long-term relationships—have cheated at least once. They have affairs but do not tell their partner.

Q How can all this work without jealousy and depression destroying our lives?

One approach is giving your relationships different priority in a hierarchy. Some relationships are secondary—a dime is not the same as a hundred dollars. But if you spread a pat of butter too thin on a slice of bread there isn't enough to go around. That's risky, too.

Q Your parting advice?

Be careful not to give up the advantage of your long-term relationship—of knowing each other, being close to each other. It's hard to achieve, but easier if you accept that love and life are not the same. When they go head-to-head, life always wins. It's easier to find someone else than a life where you can flourish. Because you need self-fulfillment, a decent marriage with enough love and the chance to personally flourish is sometimes ideal.

The deepest kind of love needs time.
~

Marriage Makes You Healthier

THE LONGEVITY BUMP OF COMMITTED LOVE

Being in a long, stable marriage can slash your risk of an early death.

Ben ran 3 miles a day and worked out with free weights. He loved his job in finance, adored his wife and kids, and was proud to look a decade younger than his 50 years. In fact, his only major complaint was that his wife of 20 years was constantly nagging him to get a checkup. But Lisa had noticed something she said was "not right" about the color in his face after a run. And her husband seemed to be a little too short of breath.

"It's just pollen!" he snapped. "There's nothing wrong with me."

Undaunted, Lisa made a doctor's appointment for Ben—and, after an argument, he finally gave in. A physical showed worrisome signs of heart disease, resulting in more testing and a procedure to open a nearly blocked artery. Lisa's observations, along with her persistent nagging, had likely saved her husband's life— and he knew it. Ben also knew he could relax after the procedure was over because Lisa would make sure he took all his medications and double-check all the doctor's instructions.

While not all examples are as dramatic as preventing a heart attack or stroke, a growing body of research has shown that being in a supportive marriage or domestic partnership and sticking it out for the long haul can provide some life-changing—and even lifesaving—health benefits.

Couples who are physically active together boost their relationship and their health.

For example, married folks often live longer (and with fewer disabilities in old age), compared to single people. A large-scale survey of death data by the Rand Corporation and Social Security researchers found a consistent survival advantage for married men and women compared to unmarried folks—married men, especially, got an extra boost of longevity.

No one knows every reason that a stable marriage may benefit health. But based on growing evidence, one thing is certain: For two of the most serious health problems, cardiovascular disease and cancer, being married can actually be good medicine.

✛ Getting to the Heart of Marriage

Heart attacks and strokes caused by cardiovascular disease result in one in four deaths of Americans each year, according to the Centers for Disease Control and Prevention. There are several known risk factors for cardiovascular disease, including high blood

Your partner can pick up on hidden dangers and health risks.

~

Support from a spouse may improve survival rates.

~

pressure, elevated cholesterol levels, being sedentary and smoking. Not being married might belong on that list, too.

An analysis of dozens of studies involving about 2 million participants documented heart disease–related events and outcomes in both married and single people. The results, published in the journal *Heart*, found marriage lowered the odds of having heart attacks and strokes. The risk of heart attack was especially elevated in those who had never married—a whopping 42 percent higher.

Although this was the largest study of its kind into how marriage may help heart health, it doesn't mean that every person who is single is doomed to have heart disease or stroke—or is even at risk. And it doesn't mean that simply having married status will automatically protect your heart health.

Instead, the research team suggests, it is the behaviors within a good marriage that likely protect individuals from heart attack and stroke. For example, married people are more likely

Partners stay
in each other's
field of vision.

Encouraging
activity helps
to keep you
both healthy.

to remind each other to take any needed medications and alert each other to potential health problems. Married partners also usually have better financial security and a stronger network of friends than unmarried people.

In addition, when married people do have heart attacks, they are 14 percent more likely to survive than their single counterparts. They even get better faster and leave the hospital two days sooner, on average, according to a study of 25,000 heart attack patients by University of East Anglia and Aston Medical School investigators.

"A heart attack can have both devastating physical and psychological effects, most of which are hidden from the outside world. These findings suggest that the support offered by a spouse can have a beneficial effect on heart-attack survivors, perhaps helping to minimize the impact of a heart attack," noted cardiologist Mike Knapton, associate medical director at the British Heart Foundation.

When heart surgery is necessary, there's more good news about the marriage and heart connection: Marriage gives adults a clear survival advantage. In fact, married adults are more than three times more likely than single people to survive the same surgery over the next three months, according to research headed by Emory University sociologist Ellen Idler.

What's more, the strong protective effect of being married lasted for up to five years following coronary artery bypass surgery, and it was equal for men and women. However, unmarried patients with the same condition and surgery were twice as likely to die.

"We found that marriage boosted survival, whether the patient was a man or a woman. The findings underscore the important role of spouses as caregivers during health crises," said Idler. "And husbands were apparently just as good at caregiving as wives."

The researchers emphasized that their findings don't mean single people should feel extra afraid of a heart attack. Instead, the researchers say, the supportive nature of other people—which seems to be more common among married folks—is likely the explanation for the better heart attack outcomes and should be considered by doctors when treating and counseling patients.

✚ Can Marriage Conquer Cancer?

Despite advances in the diagnosis and treatment of many forms of cancer, the statistics are still sobering. The American Cancer Society estimates that about 1.7 million new cases of cancer were diagnosed in the U.S. in 2019, and 606,880 people were thought to have died from the disease. While genetics, lifestyle and environmental factors all play possible roles in who develops a malignancy and who survives one, several studies show marriage may put cancer patients at an advantage.

Using data from the National Cancer Institute's surveillance, epidemiology and

A stable union can alter your underlying biology.

~

end-results program, a research team from Dana-Farber Cancer Institute and Brigham and Women's Hospital analyzed the cases of 734,889 people diagnosed with cancer over the course of four years. The scientists concentrated on the 10 leading causes of American cancer deaths: lung, colorectal, breast, pancreatic, prostate, liver/bile duct, non-Hodgkin's lymphoma, head and neck, ovarian and esophageal cancers.

They searched for factors that might influence health outcomes, including age, sex, race, education and household income. Marriage, it turned out, dramatically stood out as a factor influencing survival. Men and women who were married when diagnosed with cancer lived longer than those who were single.

> # One recent study found colon cancer patients who were married had a significantly higher 5-year survival rate.
> ~

One explanation is that married people are more likely to notice physical changes in each other that need medical attention, resulting in cancer being diagnosed at an earlier stage, when it's usually easier to treat successfully.

"Our data suggests that marriage can have a significant health impact for patients with cancer, and this was consistent among every cancer that we reviewed," said Harvard radiation oncologist Ayal Aizer. "We suspect that social support from spouses is what's driving the striking improvement in survival. Spouses often accompany patients on their visits and make sure they understand the recommendations and complete all their treatments." A partner can increase the likelihood of compliance by increasing hope, as well.

Unmarried cancer patients, on the other hand, were 17 percent more likely to have cancer that had spread and were more than 50 percent less likely to have received appropriate therapy for their malignancy. It's a worrisome finding that has implications for improving cancer treatment for everyone, married and single.

Paul Nguyen, a radiation oncologist at Dana-Farber Cancer Institute and Brigham and Women's Hospital, emphasized that the study isn't just an affirmation of health benefits in marriage. It should send a message to anyone who has a friend or loved one with cancer or another serious

Getting in sync with your partner deepens your bond.

illness. "By being there for that person and helping them navigate appointments and make it through all their treatments, you can make a real difference to that person's outcome," he said.

♣ The Partner Prescription

Could there be a biological reason that marriage boosts health? Researchers say the answer is yes. It makes sense that people in stable unions may have less psychological stress than their single counterparts, and studies support that view. Researchers found lower levels of the stress hormone cortisol in married people, compared to those who had never married or were previously married. "It is exciting to discover a physiological pathway that may explain how relationships influence health and disease," said researcher Brian Chin.

Prolonged stress triggers elevated levels of cortisol—which in turn can disrupt the body's ability to regulate inflammation, a process linked to the development and progression of cardiovascular disease and cancer.

Cortisol levels are normally highest in the morning and fall during the day, and married people's cortisol plummeted faster than that of their unmarried counterparts. It's a pattern linked to less heart disease and better survival in cancer patients, researchers noted—and another clue in explaining the healthy advantage of marriage.

HEALTH-BOOSTING MARRIAGE STRATEGIES

Living together in a committed relationship comes with some key health perks.

1 DON'T IGNORE THE SNORE

Of course you're peeved when your sleeping spouse sounds like a snorting animal, wrecking your slumber. But don't just flee to a spare room. Insist that your snoring partner be tested for sleep apnea, a potentially serious disorder marked by breathing that repeatedly stops and starts. It's a frequent cause of hypertension, raising the risk for cardiovascular problems and stroke. Snoring can also raise a nonsnoring partner's blood pressure, so treatment will be a boon to both.

2 SEARCH YOUR SPOUSE ONCE A MONTH

Giving each other's skin a monthly once-over could be lifesaving. Any

3 GET OFF THE COUCH

Regular physical activity lowers the risk for serious health problems, including cancer, heart disease and diabetes—but few Americans or their spouses get enough exercise. All it takes is for someone to make the first move. When one partner started exercising, their spouse was 40 to 70 percent more likely to do the same, according to one recent study.

changes in skin coloration could point to cancer. Pay special attention to areas your mate can't see easily see, like the top of the scalp, or back of the neck or knees. Most skin cancers are usually highly curable, but melanoma could be deadly. "If you notice any suspicious spots or anything changing, itching or bleeding, see a board-certified dermatologist," advises dermatologist Henry W. Lim.

4 GIVE EMOTIONAL SUPPORT

Living with a depressed spouse can be frustrating and damage relationships. But in addition to encouraging a depressed partner to get professional help, piling on affection can help your partner recover, according to University of Alberta research. What's more, loving support for a depressed partner today can boost the mental health of your spouse in the future.

5 SAY YES TO SOCIAL ACTIVITIES

Living in a committed long-term relationship

is known to lower the risk for mind-robbing Alzheimer's disease and other forms of dementia. In fact, the dementia risk for people who have always been single is 42 percent higher than that of those who are married, according to a recent British study. Eating healthier, and smoking and drinking less, are all associated with both marriage and lowered dementia risk, and could be part of the explanation.

Married
With Children

HAVING KIDS CAN MAKE RELATIONSHIPS MORE CHALLENGING—
BUT IT ALSO INCREASES THE STAKES FOR SUCCESS.

Most couples expect that having a baby will change their day-to-day lives, but they're often caught off guard by how much parenthood affects their relationship as well. Couples who rarely fought during their child-free years soon find themselves snapping at each other, harboring resentments and feeling less-than-loving toward each other. Confronted with this very phenomenon after welcoming her own daughter, journalist Jancee Dunn worked hard to retain love for her husband while navigating the uncharted waters of new parenthood, sharing some of her discoveries in the new book *How Not to Hate Your Husband After Kids*. She discusses some of her most important observations here.

Research shows that at least 66 percent of divorced couples in the United States are childless.

~

Q You state that tension in a marriage can shake children. How did you come to this conclusion?

I noticed that our daughter's personality was changing, and she was becoming more watchful. I assumed that if we were mad only at each other and not at her, she wouldn't be affected. We were sweet with her all the time but curt with each other, and she started to sense the dynamic and get a little subdued. That was a wake-up call.

Q You've arrived at a number of strategies to help you work on your marriage while raising a kid. Can you talk about one of the most important?

State clearly what you want. Be very specific and ask for what you need. My failing was hoping that my husband, Tom, would instinctively help me out. No! It didn't occur to me to say "Hey, please get off the couch. I need help doing x, y and z."

Q How do you and your husband share time off so that everyone gets a break?

Negotiate your weekends. We do it on Fridays (it's so boring), but if you don't ask, you might not get. Block out time for yourselves in advance—book coffee with a friend or sign up for a prepaid fitness class—and put it on the calendar, with the understanding that you'll each watch your child during the other spouse's

A happy
marriage
creates a
solid family
foundation.

An affectionate home makes children feel safe, secure, happy and loved. Remember to kiss your kids and spouse every day.

allotted free time. Both people should get a chance to do something for themselves each weekend, whether it's work or leisure. Taking even 30 minutes alone results in a parent who is less burned-out and reactive. Also— and this is extremely important to note— children's birthday parties or park playdates are parenting, not leisure time!

Q What do you do to resolve disagreements when parents have different approaches for handling the kids?
Fight fair. One of the relationship therapists we met with uses the term "full-respect living." It means that your interactions with your husband or wife should never drop below simple respect; that you can stand up for yourself and be assertive without being disrespectful to your partner. It's hard to uphold but always worth keeping in the back of one's mind. You're now the grown-ups, so fight like grown-ups. It's very beneficial for kids to see their parents work to resolve disagreements in a respectful manner.

Kids pick up on more than you think, so model mutual respect and concern.

~

Take time to connect, even if it's brief.

Q How should we approach sharing household responsibilities and tasks?

Once you have a child, you're in a brand-new relationship with a whole new set of rules, and everything is up for negotiation. Problems arise when things are not clear. We divvy up chores according to preference. I love food, so I do the grocery shopping. We used to spend a lot of time on weekend mornings arguing about who deserved to sleep in more. This amounts to wasting time by starting everything anew each day/week/month; it's ridiculous. Now we take turns sleeping in—we each get one morning per weekend—and we're no longer wasting time arguing over who works harder or who is the bigger martyr.

Q When responsibilities feel unequal and one partner has a greater burden, how do you overcome resentment?

Be generous and don't spit on the gift of time you have just given. You can't tell your spouse that it's fine to go on a weeklong work trip and then be resentful later. Give freely! Don't reflexively be resentful if it's not costing you anything.

Q How has letting go of control helped your relationship with your husband and your child?

You have to let the other person do things their own way. In the beginning, I would fix everything that Tom did with our baby and then complain that he wasn't helping. You can't have it both ways.

Q What strategies did you try that definitely did not work out for you?

Harville Hendrix's 30-day Zero Negativity Challenge, where you're not supposed to say anything negative to your partner for 30 days. We failed that one on the very first day. The challenge requires that you put frowny face stickers on the calendar, and we ran out of those stickers. That effort was a spectacular failure.

Q It's been more than two years since you began your research into shared parenting and marriage. What benefits have you noticed for your daughter over the long-term?

Our daughter has now become the most happy-go-lucky kid. Some of it is probably her innate personality, but some of it is because we have created a safe and loving environment in our house and are affectionate both to her and to each other. My husband and I are her world and her foundation, so whenever we are affectionate with each other, she gets a little happy hit, too. She pretends to be grossed out when she sees us kiss each other, but it actually makes her feel more secure. Also, the more you put these positive and proactive strategies into practice throughout your day, the easier and easier they start to become.

Q As a parting shot, can you describe the most important life lesson for protecting and nurturing a marriage while raising children?

It's easy to get caught up in the craziness of daily life with kids, but you have to think of your marriage as a third entity in all this. There are your needs, there are your partner's needs and then there are your marriage's needs. You must consider all three of these important.

PARENT VS. PARENT

When you keep differences friendly and constructive, kids will benefit.

▶▶ DON'T AVOID CONFLICT
"Not all conflict is bad—it's about how you manage it," says researcher Olena Kopystynska. Indeed, your kids face conflict all the time and must learn how to handle it.

▶▶ ELIMINATE HOSTILITY
Children intuitively pick up on the way parents interact with each other, and a hostile atmosphere can threaten their sense of safety and stability in the home, Kopystynska says. "They may not be able to express their insecurities verbally, but they can feel it."

▶▶ BE CONSTRUCTIVE
Watch your language and try to solve the problem amicably. Even in disagreement, be supportive of your partner—especially in front of your child. If your child gets involved in a dispute with you or your partner, avoid using a harsh tone and do not direct your feeling of anger or dissatisfaction at the child.

The Good Fight

PERFECTING THE ART OF
THE ARGUMENT CAN STRENGTHEN
YOUR RELATIONSHIP.

Every couple will have at least one fight over the course of their marriage. Even the happiest have disagreements from time to time. The most successful marriages are not those where the couple never argue, but instead, where partners know how to argue well.

According to relationship experts, the most important component of maintaining a strong marriage is communication. Being able to successfully convey what you are feeling (and why) to your partner will help you overcome many typical marital disagreements. California-based psychologist Stan Tatkin, author of *We Do*, suggests keeping your communications face-to-face while navigating a disagreement with your spouse. Try to maintain eye contact while talking, he says, and avoid hashing out any grievances over the telephone, through text message or via email. Much of the intent and inflection of your words can get lost in these ways, leaving too much open to interpretation.

Face-to-face
discussion can
have you seeing
each other's
point of view.

Compromise
is a key part
of conflict
resolution.

◆ Be Present and Flexible

Communicating face-to-face also allows you to observe the things that your partner is not saying, by reading his or her nonverbal cues. This allows you to adjust your approach to the topic, if you see that your partner is signaling to you that he or she has become frustrated or tense.

If you feel like you are not getting anywhere or are revisiting a well-trod topic, set a timer for your conversation. Agree to speak about the topic for a specified time, such as five minutes. At the end of the five minutes, move on to another activity, or take a break. This gives both of you time to think, reflect and gain some perspective.

When you find yourself stuck on a point of contention, ask the "why" questions. Tatkin suggests asking your spouse questions like, "Why do you or don't you want to have kids?" instead of phrasing the question in a way that does not prompt them for an explanation, such as, "Do you want to have kids?"

◆ Go for a Win-Win

If a battle becomes particularly heated or hurtful in any way, take a time-out. Before stepping deeper into the muck, back off of any discussion with your partner for several hours so that emotions can calm and the air can clear. Do not keep calling. Do not keep texting. Let anger and animosity fade before trying again.

Above all, remember that the two of you are in this together. The best outcome in any disagreement is one where both of you feel good about the results. Focus on win-win situations, not being right.

Knowing how to disagree with your partner and talking through your differences so that you both feel heard is a major component of a successful union.

RULES OF ENGAGEMENT

➻ **COMMUNICATE** your feelings without injecting negative emotions.

➻ **EXPLAIN** what you're feeling and why—without placing blame.

➻ **MAINTAIN EYE CONTACT** during a fight.

➻ **SET A TIMER** so that your disagreement has an ending, even if unresolved.

➻ **WALK AWAY** before things get ugly.

➻ **AVOID CRUELTY** You will not be able to take back anything you say, so never say anything that can cause harm.

Complex Relations

YOU CAN PROTECT YOUR MARRIAGE BY GETTING ALONG WITH THE IN-LAWS—BUT SET SOME LIMITS FIRST.

When you get married, you're suddenly thrust into an existing family with complicated dynamics that you have to learn to navigate (with your partner's help). Conflicts will inevitably arise, and the main source of all this tension boils down to one little word: *in-law*.

"In-laws are often competing for your partner's time, love and attention," explains social psychologist Susan Newman, author of *The Book of No*. You may have plans with your spouse for just the two of you, and suddenly your in-laws need help

Include extended family in your leisure plans.

with a task, or want everyone to come over for the weekend. As partners try to figure out how to divide their time among all their new responsibilities, in-laws can feel neglected or even shut out of their child's life, which can be destructive for the entire family, Newman warns.

Other factors can also put a strain on a couple's relationships with in-laws. Resentment can build when in-laws intrude on the couple's life together by visiting unannounced or doing chores without being asked. In-laws can be hurt when a couple eschews a long-standing family tradition in favor of their own goals and desires or when they disagree with the way their child and his or her spouse raises their grandchildren—or even keeps their house.

Why should we care so much about how we relate to in-laws, who live separate lives, often thousands of miles away? A seminal study published in the *Journal of Marriage and Family* in 2001 examined the association between discord with in-laws and marital satisfaction. The findings? Participants' relationships with

Get along with the in-laws, for a happier union.
~

their in-laws predicted their happiness with their marriage. In other words, your relationship with your in-laws can influence your relationship with your spouse, creating problems between you and your partner that challenge your intimacy and

Set boundaries about how much you share with your in-laws.

1 Give In-Laws Alone Time With Their Child

Jealousy is very common in the in-law relationship. As Newman points out, the son- or daughter-in-law has "essentially taken the in-laws' baby away." Giving your partner time with their parents apart from you shows understanding and helps appease that little green monster, which could otherwise damage your relationship.

2 Stay Away From Topics That You Know Will Push Buttons

From politics and religion to child-rearing decisions, avoid bringing up any subjects that you know are bound to raise tensions. Conflict can't be prevented completely, but you can do your part to identify the sore spots and quit needling them.

3 Ask Your In-Laws for Their Help

"People want to feel needed," Newman says, adding that one of the best ways to bond with your in-laws is to seek their advice or expertise. Maybe your in-law knows a lot about being a homeowner and you're looking into buying your first house. Not only will your in-law feel proud to share their experience with you, but you'll also gain some valuable tips from someone who has been there and done that.

strain your family life. For the sake of your and your partner's well-being, don't let that happen.

Here are six steps you can take to protect your marriage and deflate any tension before it turns too toxic.

> ### *Don't limit your time together to the holidays, which inherently bring their own added stress.*
> ~

4 Say No—And Set Boundaries
The thought of saying "no" to your in-laws is terrifying. However, Newman warns, when you don't set boundaries, "you're essentially adding more tension to the relationship, because you're going to be quietly fuming." Couples often don't realize they have the power to say no to a request or situation, and that most in-laws will adapt their needs in order to stay close with their child and/or grandchildren.

5 Make Sure Your In-Laws Are Up-to-Date on Your Family's Current Events
It's tempting to put talking to your in-laws about major changes in your life on the back burner so you don't have to deal with their unsolicited opinions, which may differ from your own perspective. But when your in-laws find out the big news in some other way, they're going to feel betrayed that you didn't tell them first. The key is to let your partner take the lead. They know their own parents better than you do, Newman explains, and will have a better grasp of when and how to tell them. Plus, if your in-laws don't take the news well, being the messenger will just send unwarranted blame your way.

6 Remember That Your Primary Relationship Is With Your Spouse, Not Your Parents
According to Karl Pillemer, professor of human development at Cornell University: "In a conflict between your spouse and your family, support your spouse. You must present a united front to your families, making it clear from the beginning that your spouse comes first. In couples where this allegiance does not happen, marital problems swiftly follow. In fact, some of the bitterest disputes occur over a spouse's failure to support his or her partner."

You may have heard the saying that in-laws aren't losing a child but gaining one. This sentiment doesn't always reflect real life. But by keeping the suggestions above in mind, you can build happier relationships with your in-laws—and protect your marriage as the most sacred and important relationship in your life.

When you can't be
together in person,
keep the lines of
communication open.

Feathering the Empty Nest

WHEN CHILDREN LEAVE HOME, SOME PARENTS REVEL
IN THEIR NEWFOUND FREEDOM WHILE OTHERS
FEEL UNMOORED. HERE'S HOW TO REBUILD.

The luckiest parents will face the day their children fly the coop—after all, who would want it any other way? We all want to launch our kids, healthy and whole, into the world! Here, psychologist Suzanne Degges-White, an expert in life transitions at Northern Illinois University, discusses how parents can come together, regain their footing, remake their lives and find their passions once the children have left home.

Q What are the most common emotional responses a couple has to the empty nest?

It seems that there are two polar-opposite sets of expectations about an impending empty nest. On one end, there are couples who are eagerly awaiting the freedom that an empty nest will allow. They see this as a new opportunity to get to know each other again and to be able to make plans without having to take anyone into consideration beyond themselves. Then there are those couples who are dreading the emptiness they feel will fill the house once their child departs. They worry about the lack of companionship or the change in their own identities that will arrive when their parenting roles begin to ebb. What can be surprising is when couples who are expecting loneliness and a feeling of bereavement are pleasantly surprised by how much they enjoy the now-empty house, or how much freer they feel to change up their routines. And, at the other end of the spectrum, those couples who were counting the days until they had their home all to themselves might be surprised at how lonesome their home now feels.

Q What are the benefits to a couple who now has an empty nest?

There's a new sense of freedom that the "adults" can enjoy in their home now. While most adolescents seem to lead a relatively autonomous life, now you *really* can stop worrying about a lot of little things you might not have even realized you were worrying about—leaving on the porch light, figuring out how many places to set at the table, which days are game days, who needs the car, etc.

Q How can you explore your own sense of self?

With all the children out of the house, you are able to explore your own personal identity. Hobbies and leisure pursuits don't have to be scheduled around child-related commitments—and you don't have to wonder who took the fresh can of tennis balls or if the book-club schedule conflicts with game nights. Focus on the joy of knowing that you and your partner are free to enjoy intimacy without a child showing up unexpectedly.

Q What are the challenges for a couple faced with an empty nest?

When the last child leaves home, there can be a lot of dissonance. It can be disconcerting when being a mother or a father is a huge part of your identity but there are no longer any children in the house to parent. Warning: Don't let yourself suddenly try to parent your partner, younger colleagues at work, and so on. Parenting isn't a "one-size-parents-all" proposition—and your attempts to parent other adults may cost you some goodwill from others.

Having the house
to yourself can
feel liberating.

99

Forgotten pleasures:
coffee and reading a
paper on the balcony.

Q How do couples deal with the sense of loss?

Grief is a natural response. It's OK if you need to spend some time sitting in your child's now-empty room and take a short ride down memory lane. It's normal to miss your child, but it's not normal to obsess about their absence or let your grief get in the way of daily activities. It's normal to hold on to a child's favorite blankie or sports jersey; it's not normal to hold that blankie or jersey on a regular basis!

Q A big challenge of the empty nest is that it is often accompanied by other transitions. How does that work?

Caregiving for older adult relatives may now be needed. Job transitions may be upcoming —either stepping down at work, retiring or beginning a new job hunt now that the kids are grown and out of the house. Sometimes it's not just the effect of one transition, a child moving out; it can be the combined effect of multiple transitions and losses at one time that makes the empty nest such a painful experience. Empty nesters may also feel that this is a milestone in the aging process. As the children mature and grow up, their parents are also maturing—but it's a time when our culture would consider their aging and development as growing old, not growing up. This can be a rude

awakening for some people as they realize their primary parental role has downshifted into a brand-new life stage.

Q When the children are no longer there for a couple to focus on, how can the couple come back to being closer to each other? How can they fill the space left between them?

This can be a difficult time for many couples —especially today, when our culture has enthusiastically embraced the notion of child-focused parenting so completely. For many couples facing a newly empty nest, this period puts them at a loss as to how to fill their leisure time. Calendars without kids' activities

Take the time to rebuild your life as a pair.

~

scheduled into them can seem hopelessly empty. However, this is the time when the calendar can now be populated with shared activities between partners. If you feel that you and your partner have grown apart—a feeling that a lot of people admit to once their kids have all moved out—then it's essential that you focus on an activity or pastime that can help to bring the two of you back together.

Q What about trying new things?
Some couples will decide to pursue an activity that neither partner has tried before. This might be a sport, such as biking or golf; a hobby, like baking or French cooking; or a commitment to a healthier lifestyle, in terms of diet and exercise. If there used to be a regular game night or activity schedule when your child was at home, choose that night to schedule a shared activity with your partner. You'll be able to fill that hole and keep up in the habit of blocking off that time on your calendar. There should also be many new opportunities for

conversation and sharing between partners. This can be a positive development in many ways—but it might make for some awkward and silent mealtimes in the beginning. Once a couple have asked each other about their days, the conversation can fall flat. Challenge each other to commit to listening and engaging with each other during meals. Find some topics that interest both of you and relearn the skillful art of shared communication. If there's a cause that really excites you, encourage your partner to get involved in cause-related activities. You've worked together for 18-plus years to raise your child—now you can find another positive way to work together for a good cause.

Q What can a couple do to make their relationship better than ever, once they have an empty nest?
Some couples bounce right back when the last child heads out, but most end up at a loss once the reality of the smaller family footprint truly sets in. To successfully navigate that transition, acknowledge that time and experience have transformed your relationship. If either of you believes that the effects have been less than positive, be sure to openly address those concerns. Until you admit that there might be a problem, you can't work together to find a workable solution.

Q Can couples ever get back to the way they were at the start of their relationship?

While sometimes it can be unsettling for a couple to realize that they related to each other primarily through their kids, it's also an opportunity to enjoy that feeling of novelty and newness that early relationships typically offer. Getting to know your partner all over again can be surprisingly enjoyable when you think of it as renewing your relationship, even if it sometimes feels like "rewiring" an old relationship. Talk about what drew you to each other in the first place when your relationship was just beginning. This helps you get back into the mindset of romantic partners, not just co-parents. Find a way to share with each other every day. You can make a commitment to having dinner chats and breakfast conversations, taking daily walks without the cellphones—whatever is going to work for your schedule. Make the commitment as sacrosanct as you possibly can.

Q What about the physical space a child has left behind?

Satisfy the desire to fill the space in your daily life or in the home with a literal filling of the space by redecorating the room where your child once slept. Turn that empty bedroom into a home gym with a variety of fitness equipment. Or, if exercise is not your thing, consider other options, such as creating a photography darkroom, a studio for your painting or crafting or a media room that's complete with reclining theater seats, speakers and a giant screen. Or maybe build yourself a new home office to embark on a second career or volunteer work. Be open to new ideas, and consider the additional space in your life as an invitation to be more generative and creative than ever before.

Q What should couples avoid?

Don't sweat the small stuff—without a child in the house to receive your focused attention, little irritants may suddenly start to become a lot more significant than they should be. Don't assume that your partner wants to be the recipient of the attention you once gave your child. Instead, find a hobby or activity where you can channel some of that newfound time and energy. Don't be surprised if the transition is difficult—or if it isn't! Everyone handles this life transition differently, and it's OK to feel euphoric or grief-stricken (for a little while—then you need to pick yourself up). Don't make a snap decision about your relationship with your partner, even if things feel rough. Just because the last kid has moved out doesn't mean you must go, too.

5 STEPS FOR SUCCESS
ONCE THE KIDS ARE GROWN

With the gift of time, nurture your relationship and pursue your personal dreams. By making healthy adjustments after your child leaves home, you can learn to embrace your new phase of life and forge an even closer connection with your intimate partner.

The empty nest is a cliché—and, as positive psychology life coach Caren Osten points out, it isn't really true. "There are still parents in the nest once the children have left," says Osten. It can feel bewildering for spouses who have spent so many years as parents to suddenly find themselves right back where they started. But that doesn't mean the parents will feel sad; empty nesters can find it liberating to have time to pursue their own interests, desires and dreams. Here's how to navigate the empty nest and avoid its pitfalls.

1
Consistently schedule time for activities as a couple, such as meals out, concerts, morning bike rides and weekend museum visits.

2
Vocally communicate your feelings about your empty nest to your partner so that they don't interpret your sadness as marital anger or disappointment. Openly expressing how you are feeling can evoke empathy from your partner, thereby sparking increased intimacy.

3
Try a new hobby together, like learning bridge, taking a cooking class or joining a movie club.

4
Avoid judging your partner. Instead, ask how they're feeling about this new phase of life and give them room to have their own reactions to their child leaving home.

5
Bring fun and play back into your romantic lives to help rekindle your old connection.

CHAPTER 3

Perfecting the Union

ENDLESS LOVE:
ENDURING COUPLES EXPLAIN
HOW TO KEEP THE TALK, THE FUN
AND THE SEX GOING FOR DECADES.

Spice It Up

HOW TO KEEP HAVING GREAT SEX.

Stay in any relationship long enough, and eventually your sex life, no matter how spicy it was at the start, will peter out. How and when it does so varies with everyone. For some couples, the spark vanishes in under a year, while for others it can endure for ages. That flameout may manifest as a drop, slow or sudden, in the frequency of physical intimacy. Or it may come as a decline in the self-perceived quality of your sex life. Other times, a sex life can come to a complete halt. Often, the drag on a sex life can include elements from all these columns—and many other impediments as well.

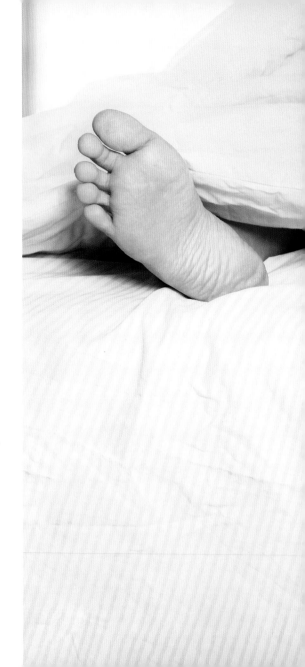

1
Don't fixate on one type
of outcome, like penetrative
intercourse or orgasm.
Try making out or fooling
around—or banning orgasms
to focus only on intimacy.

GREAT
SEX
TIP

2

Open up to your partner about desires you've never shared or new desires as they arise. You may be surprised at how willing they are to accommodate your hidden needs and interests.

3

Find ways to work more casual touch and physical closeness into your life. Simple acts of physical connection, even if they're not sexual, can help with a sense of attachment to a partner. Cuddle on the couch, hold hands walking down the street or (if you can) touch each other as you sleep.

This isn't just general wisdom. Relationship researchers recognize this phenomenon—some even dub it "the intimacy-desire paradox"—and studies document that it is widespread.

In some ways, a dip in desire isn't entirely bad. If we spent our lives in the throes of the kind of passion many experience at the start of a relationship, other writers have quipped, we'd never get anything done. But at a certain point, for many, it becomes distressing—and understandably so.

"When sex is consensual, pleasurable and enjoyable, it helps us feel closer and connected to our partner," explains sex researcher Sarah Hunter Murray.

It also "contributes to overall quality of life," adds Rachel Needle, a psychologist, sex therapist and co-director of the Modern Sex Therapy Institutes. On top of that, American culture,

especially, paints an active sex life as the key to any functional relationship; endless songs, shows and movies glorify the quest to "get that spark back."

Fortunately, most relationship experts agree: Sexual nadirs don't have to be permanent. It is entirely possible to maintain or reignite old sparks and keep having great sex well into a relationship. But to understand how to maintain a satisfying sex life in a long-term relationship, one has to understand what leads sex to fizzle out in the first place—a trickier task than you might suspect.

✦ Need for Novelty

Common wisdom (and a slew of studies and relationship advice articles) holds that humans are hardwired to react to novelty and surprise. Newness gives us a dopamine rush that really gets things steamy. Relationships are often the opposite of that. Familiarity and routine sabotage intimacy.

GREAT
SEX
TIP

4

Try to establish a sense of egalitarianism in your relationship. This doesn't have to mean splitting every task in half. But making sure one partner doesn't feel overburdened—and that both members of the relationship are in it together—can remove a roadblock to physical intimacy.

Age seems like it should play a role as well. Male sex drive peaks at around age 18, claims biological anthropologist Helen Fisher; for women, the peak is more like 25. As testosterone, the hormone that seems to control desire, drops off—especially in middle age—so does the desire for, and the level of effort we put into, sex.

Many people report a lack of interest in sex, adds sex sociologist Edward Laumann, because they have trouble with having penetrative sex. For men, that usually means erectile dysfunction (ED). For women, that may mean vaginal dryness or other issues that can make copulation painful. The longer one stays in a relationship, it stands to reason, the more our bodies will sabotage our once-steamy sex lives.

Life is never that clear-cut, though. Fisher has studied a number of couples who, despite being together for decades, still profess deep romantic love for each other—and likely, she notes, still have solid sex lives, familiarity be damned. Some people, she adds, just have naturally high sex drives that don't dip as readily over time. Women often actually experience a boost in sex drive in middle age because, as Fisher points out, "in menopause, levels of estrogen go down a great deal and levels of testosterone go down but not to the same extent, so testosterone, which is the sex hormone in both men and women, becomes more visible" in them. Laumann also points out that some seemingly unhealthy people still maintain a great deal of sexual desire and functionality.

"While sexual frequency does tend to decline as we age, patterns of sexual activity aren't linear and there are many aspects of life, beyond physiological functioning, that affect interest in sexual activity," says women's health researcher Tamar Krishnamurti.

GREAT SEX TIP

5

Voice your desire for each other. Maybe even make it a point to do so at least once a day. It always helps to know that you and your partner still want each other, even if your sex life is on the rocks.

GREAT
SEX
TIP

6
Make sure
you and your
partner have a
sense of autonomy
so that you see
yourselves as
more than just a
couple. Having the
space to be an
individual can be
enough to help
your sex life.

7

**Establish open lines of communication in your relationship.
Be sure both of you are responsive to each other's needs to minimize
the risk of lingering or unspoken conflicts that can sap desire.**

In early 2018, researchers Julie Lasslo and Kristen Mark conducted a meta-analysis of more than five dozen studies on sex in long-term relationships conducted over the past two decades. They found that a host of idiosyncratic and often transient personal, interpersonal and social variables all seem to affect our intimate lives. Work and life stress, unresolved arguments, the distractions of children, and other factors may sap away the time for sex or leave us too anxious, depressed or physically and emotionally drained to really get into it. (Antidepressants, used by some 13 percent of Americans, often take a toll on sex drive as well.) The sheer number of variables at play, physically and mentally, Laumann points out, makes it all but impossible for anyone to predict how sex in a given relationship will play out over time.

The important thing, Needle says, is to recognize that these factors are unpleasant but common—and not a sign of failure. They "don't mean your relationship is doomed."

♣ Going With the Flow

Recognizing that sex may ebb and flow with life circumstances gives us the freedom to accept these dynamic shifts at times and not stress out about relighting the fire with a partner. "If there are some obvious external stresses, such as having a child, starting a new job, house renovations, an illness or a death in the family," explains Murray, "it may be better to accept that life is in flux and your sex life is taking a bit of a back seat" for a while. "Worrying or fixating on your sex life," she adds, "may just increase the stress or pressure instead," hurting a relationship in the long run.

Some couples may even be able to accept a permanent drop in, or end to, sex. "There shouldn't be any pressure to change behavior that's working for everyone," notes Krishnamurti.

GREAT
SEX
TIP

8

Use erectile dysfunction drugs, lubrication, relaxation techniques and other interventions to help with any apparent, immediate physiological barriers to sex or sexual pleasure. And be sure to keep talking with your partner about these issues as they arise over time.

The point is not to dwell on comparisons to others. These sexual slides become a problem only when one or both members of a relationship believes they're a problem. If you or your partner has trouble accepting a sexual status quo or finding solutions to it and talking about it, this can lead to general relationship tension, hurt feelings and even infidelity or a breakup.

But if you and your partner can acknowledge that the sexual dynamics of a relationship aren't working for at least one of you and agree that both of you want to work on increasing the quality or frequency of your sex, then you can start to figure out what to do about that nagging relationship issue.

Sometimes this means figuring out what underlying physical, social, personal or interpersonal issues are affecting your sex life and dealing with them. Any number of life

changes could be in order: Address conflicts between the two of you. Try to be more communicative. Change your diet. Dump toxic people from your life. Switch up your job.

"If you're looking to figure out what is negatively impacting your sex lives"—and what interventions you might want to try— "talk with your partner about when you started to notice a difference," says Murray. Then try to come to a common understanding about when a change occurred in your intimate lives and what may have been behind it.

The catch is that many people might not be aware of all the variables at play in their sex lives, Laumann points out. And "there isn't always a 'quick fix'" to some deeper issues, Needle adds.

But Fisher argues that you can still rekindle your sex life without addressing every issue that may affect it. She and other doctors, therapists

GREAT SEX TIP

9

Masturbate to explore your own body and pleasure. Share your insights with your partner.

AN ODE TO REGULAR SEX

Sex doesn't just feel good; it also boosts health and energy and helps us fight disease.

The benefits of sex are various and legion. Maintaining a regular sex life can help us live healthier, happier lives and bond us to our partners. And sex is self-reinforcing, so the more pleasurable, satisfying sex we have, the more we will want to have it as well. But it does more than just feel good (or great!). Consider these helpful side benefits of sex:

ENHANCED HEALTH AND WELLNESS

Sex stimulates the immune system, potentially helping people avoid infection and illnesses—although sex alone is almost certainly no replacement for eating right, staying active and getting sufficient sleep. Regular orgasms can help women tone their pelvic floor muscles, improving bladder control later in life. And regular ejaculatory orgasms seem to reduce men's risk of getting prostate cancer. Sex with others (as opposed to masturbation) also helps to lower blood pressure.

ADDED ENERGY

For most people, genital stimulation activates the dopamine system in the brain, and that "gives you energy, optimism and focus," explains biological anthropologist Helen Fisher.

MORE INTIMACY

Sex and orgasm release oxytocin, a hormone that promotes feelings of attachment to a partner we are with, as well as a sense of comfort and calm—helping, in many cases, to strengthen relationships while at least temporarily cutting stress.

PAIN RELIEF

Sexual activity releases endorphins that can help ease some suffering with pain.

BURNED CALORIES AND A REAL WORKOUT

Sex is an effective form of exercise—especially more acrobatic sessions.

HELP WITH SLEEPING THROUGH THE NIGHT

Orgasm releases prolactin, a hormone associated with a good night's sleep.

Think back on the things you found attractive about your partner when you first got together—the things they did or that you did together that got you hot and bothered. See if you can refocus on those traits—if they still work for you—or bring elements of those activities back into your life.

and sociologists have developed a number of tips and tricks for stimulating desire and mixing things up for everyone who feels like they're in a rut, regardless of their life context. (See the "Great Sex Tips" sprinkled throughout this story for some ideas.)

✤ Reigniting the Spark

Not every tip or trick will work for every couple. But all efforts to rekindle the sexual spark in a relationship share one common feature: They require time, energy and focus.

Things like scheduling sex or having daily check-ins with a partner may seem daunting or unsexy. But taking pressure off yourself and not insisting that you have to do things in exactly the right way, can help, says Fisher. Maintaining desire and intimacy, she adds, is like maintaining our bodies through exercise: It may feel tough at

first. But keep at it, and eventually it will become an enjoyable part of your life.

Sometimes the problem is so entrenched and deeply upsetting to a couple that they may decide to move on and try again with other partners. Just because sex has become irreconcilable with one person doesn't mean the experience will be the same every time out.

But most couples can pull out of a sexual rut and reestablish the spark. Sometimes they may need help figuring out what is affecting them—or they may need to work through some longtime feelings of anger, betrayal and hurt. In those cases, Needle says, they should "make an appointment with a mental health professional who specializes in sex and relationships—the sooner, the better." Don't let a sexual impasse ruin your long-standing marriage or partnership, when the problem is fixable if handled with love.

The Art of the Orgasm

LIKE DANCING OR ROCK MUSIC,
A TRUE ORGASM CAN INDUCE A TRANCE
WHERE PARTNERS LOSE EACH OTHER
IN A SHARED, DRIVING RHYTHM.

About 46 percent
of women say they
climax every time
or almost every
time they have sex.

119

Fatigue and stress can often interfere with sexual pleasure.

Jim Pfaus still remembers his first orgasm. "It was some sort of mystical event. My body had never done that before. I wanted to know, why did it happen? Why did it feel good?" he says.

As an 11-year-old growing up in the early 1970s, however, he had no idea what an orgasm was or what it meant. Pfaus began talking to his friends about it; all of them reported similar sensations. It wasn't until he took a college class on human sexuality that Pfaus learned exactly what an orgasm was. Now a behavioral neurobiologist at Concordia University in Montreal, Pfaus continues to study sexual desire. People like to ask him, "What's the best way to have an orgasm?", and his response is simple: Get into your own body and find out.

Though they vary from person to person and from orgasm to orgasm, neurobiologists have begun to focus on some of the constants. For one,

Orgasm becomes a seizure-like state when pleasure takes hold.

~

there's pleasure. For another, there's rhythm. Despite the intense focus on the former, it's the latter that has most fascinated Northwestern University psychologist Adam Safron. And it's this rhythm, from the music in the background to the pattern of physical stimulation to the firing of neurons, that may sit at the center of the orgasm.

"This rhythm creates a trance state that crowds out other things in your awareness," he explains. "Rhythms are fundamental to sex. Every aspect of the mating process is rhythmic, the whole way through."

✦ Why Do We Have Orgasms?

If Safron's theory is correct, it could help explain one of the mysteries that philosophers and scientists alike have argued about: What's the point of an orgasm, anyway?

Some of the earliest work in this area wasn't by Alfred Kinsey or Masters and Johnson, but instead by researchers who weren't even studying sex. In 1960, psychiatrist Richard Chessick documented the "Pharmacogenic Orgasm" in heroin users, all of whom experienced a surge of euphoria as they injected the drug. Over the years, researchers have also uncovered people who have orgasms while brushing their teeth or even while just thinking about sex. Finally, some individuals with epilepsy can experience a preseizure aura that feels remarkably like the moments leading up to orgasm.

"Orgasm is very much a seizure-like state," Pfaus explains, pointing out that some people with epilepsy can't have an orgasm without triggering a seizure.

It was this last fact that first led Safron to start developing his hypothesis. Like Pfaus, Safron studied sexual behavior and desire, but his expertise wasn't in neurobiology. Still, first-year neuroscience classes taught him that a rhythmic stimulus leads to rhythmic brain activity, which really grabs our attention. Whether it's dancing, running or sex, the rhythms involved push out extraneous thoughts as pleasure takes hold. Keep going, and the person can fall into a trance. Nor is the relationship between rhythm and sex limited to humans; it exists throughout the animal kingdom.

When a male fruit fly wants to get it on with a female, he performs a mating dance, meant to show off his good genes and freedom from parasites. Some birds perform a similar ritual. In fish that fertilize their eggs externally, the male will sidle up to the female, moving around in a specific pattern until she releases her eggs and he fertilizes them with a cloud of sperm. Reproduction, then, is a fundamentally rhythmic process. Mating has multiple steps, and each has its own unique cadence.

"It's all about rhythm, and there are probably optimal rhythms that make orgasm more or less likely," Pfaus says.

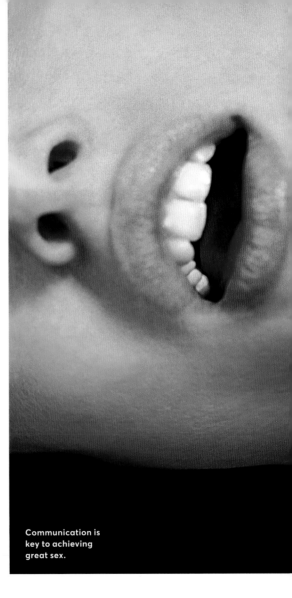

Communication is key to achieving great sex.

Erotic thoughts can contribute significantly to sexual arousal.

~

✤ Orgasm Is an Altered State

Humans, in particular, can lose themselves in one another's rhythms, which can be reflected in patterns of neuronal firing, a process known as entrainment. At its extremes, entrainment can lead to epileptic seizures when the brain's neurons fire en masse. Dial it down just a little, however, and you might see what happens during orgasm as individuals enter a trancelike state that Safron describes as an altered state of consciousness. This entrainment doesn't always happen. Just as a runner can find herself blissfully soaring over the pavement one day and slogging on asphalt the next, sexual pleasure doesn't always blot out daily concerns. If a person can't become lost in the experience, it blocks the way to orgasm.

That an orgasm doesn't always happen may explain part of its allure, says Diana Fleischman, an evolutionary psychologist at the University of Portsmouth in the U.K. Researchers call it the slot machine theory. "It's so variable and random that it becomes more reinforcing when it happens," she says.

The pleasurable afterglow of the big moment isn't just a prelude to sleep. The surge of the neurochemicals dopamine and oxytocin that accompanies orgasm helps to connect us to our partners, which reinforces them as the source of our intense pleasure. Cuddling, too, adds to the social bond between sexual partners.

"Orgasm isn't just about sex. It's about humanness. It's how we connect to each other," Safron says.

Psychophysiologist Nicole Prause of Liberos points out that although existing evidence provides some support for Safron's hypothesis, it still hasn't been tested. And doing that testing is hard, since you need to provoke the same response over and over and over again, often in the tight confines of an MRI machine.

"I don't think we know much about the neurobiology of orgasm," Prause says.

Safron and Pfaus agree that scientists know relatively little about an experience that is central to the process that keeps our species alive—and Safron hopes his work provides new avenues to explore. Regardless of what he learns, it's become clear that there isn't one right way to have an orgasm. Instead, the goal is to enjoy it and savor it as it comes, even if you can't re-create that magic moment every time.

37 percent of women say they need clitoral stimulation to achieve orgasm.

~

BIOLOGY OF THE FEMALE ORGASM
AND THE ROOTS OF DESIRE

Barry Komisaruk, a behavioral neuroscientist at Rutgers University and co-author of *The Orgasm Answer Guide*, discusses his findings on female sexual arousal.

Q Are there different paths to orgasm?

A Every woman is wired differently. Some women have a greater cluster of nerves in the clitoris, while others have more in the perineum or at the mouth of the cervix. Clitoral orgasms seem to rely on the pudendal nerve, which carries signals from the genitals, while vaginal orgasms are linked to the pelvic nerve.

Q What happens to the brain when the clitoris or the vagina is stimulated?

A It starts a cascade that is like a symphony orchestra because so many different systems become activated. Genital stimulation sends a signal to your limbic system, which is the emotional control center of the brain and includes the hippocampus, the seat of memory and fantasies, and the amygdala, which governs sexual functioning. Basically, all the major brain systems become activated at orgasm, releasing neurotransmitters like dopamine, oxytocin and serotonin, which fire up pleasure circuitry in the brain. The cerebellum becomes activated; this part of the brain is involved in movement coordination and muscle tension. The hypothalamus controls the release of hormones like oxytocin, the hormone that cements the bond between mother and child. Dopamine stimulates the nucleus accumbens, an area of the brain that responds intensely to pleasurable substances, like nicotine, caffeine and chocolate

Q Does releasing oxytocin help bind us to our mates?

A There is no evidence that if you administer oxytocin you will get romantic feelings. If you inject oxytocin in prairie voles—who are known to mate for life—they huddle together. But it could be that it increases heat loss, not that it makes them more romantic.

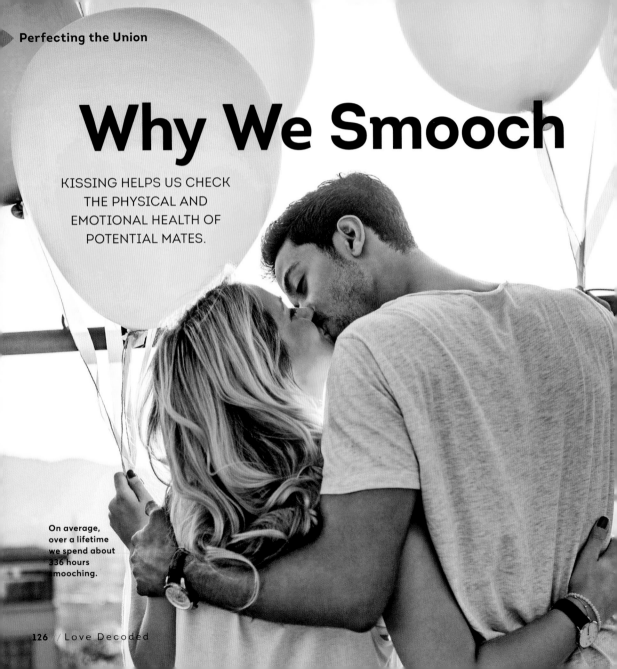

Why We Smooch

KISSING HELPS US CHECK
THE PHYSICAL AND
EMOTIONAL HEALTH OF
POTENTIAL MATES.

On average,
over a lifetime
we spend about
336 hours
smooching.

The romantic kiss starts with a glance or a touch, then the leaning in, followed by the meeting of lips. Kisses are generally pleasurable, which is why 90 percent of us remember the details of our first kiss. The practice, the hallmark of every Hollywood rom-com, is so common that it's found in about half of all cultures worldwide.

Anthropologists and evolutionary biologists have two competing theories for why humans first started smooching. One holds that a kiss provides a test-drive for potential mates. Are they attentive? Do they appear to be free from pathogens? Are they generally compatible?

The other theory contends that romantic kissing evolved from kiss-feeding. Baby birds chirp, mouths agape, and their parents regurgitate food into their waiting beaks. Human mothers do something similar with their babies: the kiss as an expression of maternal love transformed over the years into a display of sexual passion.

Scientists have studied romantic kissers during the act. At the Center for Lifespan Psychology at the Max Planck Institute for Human Development in Berlin, researchers measured kissers' brainwaves through electroencephalogram (EEG). The conclusion: During the kiss, brain activity spikes and harmonizes; the higher the synchrony, the better the self-reported quality of the kiss, as if partners were tuning forks seeking to resonate together, not just for the length of the kiss but for a longer stint in life.

Other researchers have found that kissing generates a pleasing chemical cocktail, including higher levels of feel-good serotonin; oxytocin, the attachment hormone; and dopamine, which can induce a sense of pleasure in the same brain areas as opioids. The loving, pleasurable, addictive nature of a good kiss is biologically guaranteed.

As with orgasm, one primary requirement is the ability to match rhythms with your partner, says psychologist Adam Safron of Northwestern University. "There's a reason we like to kiss. It's an intensely focused time, and you lose yourself in an intensely pleasurable experience," he says. "You become lost in the other person's rhythm." This rhythm hints at the potential for even more passion to come, which is part of its allure.

Although 90 percent of cultures kiss, only about half kiss romantically. For some, it's seen as disgusting, silly and unhygienic. That makes sense: With each romantic kiss, some 80 million bacteria are exchanged. But it continues. Kissing helps us evaluate a partner's compatibility—and likely aids in picking up on their health or genetic fitness through taste and smell. For women, the act can be essential: In cultures that favor couples over extended family, it's crucial to make sure that a partner is solid and lasting.

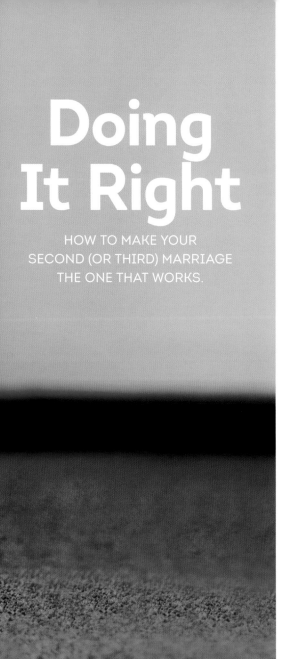

Doing It Right

HOW TO MAKE YOUR SECOND (OR THIRD) MARRIAGE THE ONE THAT WORKS.

Mary got married fresh out of college. Her husband was a few years older, and she assumed she'd spend the rest of her life with him. After all, he was exactly what she wanted in a husband—at least, that's what she thought at the time.

"I didn't really understand the complexity of relationships. I was an only child and probably a bit selfish," she recalls. "I wanted to be with someone who thought like me, who believed I was beautiful and who would take care of me."

Two children and 20 years later, the marriage ended in divorce—like about half of all marriages in the United States. Mary blames it on bad decisions, the spouses putting each other at the bottom of their priority lists and the toll of her husband's clinical depression.

♣ An Unexpected Love

Post-divorce, she threw herself into supporting herself and her two kids, working as a journalist and then in the editorial division of a large university. Marrying again was not on her "to-do" list.

Then unexpected fireworks happened. Mary traveled to a childhood friend's Fourth of July party in another city. Her friend said Mary would enjoy meeting Dale, describing him as "a hippie free spirit, a long-haired type who makes tie-dyed T-shirts." She added that he wasn't serious relationship material—after all, he was about a decade younger than Mary —but he might be fun for a one-night fling.

"That sounded pretty good to me, after the loneliness of the past few years, a failed marriage and not wanting to get back into something serious," Mary recalls. The unlikely duo not only had fun that evening, but after Mary returned to her home in another state, they began long nightly phone conversations and discovered that beyond their physical attraction, they had deep mutual interests. A month later, the young man took a bus to Mary's city, arriving with tie-dyed T-shirts in hand and his clothes packed in a drum. He rented a room near her home and found handyman work, and their relationship blossomed.

The age difference and different career paths didn't deter either of them, and he eventually moved in with Mary. This was not the match either had envisioned years before, but they found themselves happily compatible and supportive of each other (Mary jokes that coming home from work to Dale's delicious home cooking was a big perk).

The initial resentment of Mary's children faded when Dale made no attempt to replace their dad but became a friend and big brother figure instead. When Dale moved away temporarily to learn the welding trade, Mary realized how much she missed him.

Financial transparency is essential. You must disclose income, investments and debt.

"Still, it took us more than five years of living together before we got married. I'd said I was never going to get married again. And then he decided he didn't want to. It was back and forth for a while, and then we just decided to go for it," Mary says. "It made our commitment more real."

Department of the Treasury — In
U.S. Individual I
31, 2018, or other tax year beg
ial

So why is Mary's second marriage happy, despite such obvious differences between herself and her mate? Besides enjoying the same activities and each other's company, Mary says she's mellowed over the years—she's doesn't become so angry or critical when they disagree.

Clearly express your needs and make sure they can be met.

~

Mary has also learned from her husband's calmer approach to arguments. "Dale told me once, he seeks 'homeostasis.' He believes in talking things out and not going to bed angry," she says. And after spending years having adventures and living a freewheeling lifestyle, Dale treasures being part of a family. He even built Mary's father an apartment in their home and is helping to care for the elderly man.

"I am happy being married again," Mary says. "But first, I had to take a breath and say, 'OK, I can try this, it's worth the risk.' Now I can't imagine life without my husband."

✦ Why Marriages Work— or Don't—The Second Time Around

Of course, remarriage—or any marriage, if you look at divorce statistics—is a risk. But countless couples keep walking down the aisle yet again, hoping to get it right a second or even third time. In fact, about four in 10 marriages include at least one partner who has tied the knot before, and in two in 10 couples, both partners have been

A mellower attitude can bring success.

~

Second marriages often involve mixing families and belongings, and combining or moving homes.

previously married, according to the Pew Research Center.

Unfortunately, the divorce rate for the second or third marriage is even higher than the first—but why? Emory University clinical psychologist Rachel Hershenberg, author of *Activating Happiness*, says one key reason is that people are afraid to ask for what they really want and need in a relationship. And it can be especially difficult to speak up if your self-esteem has been clobbered in a divorce and you fear rejection or another failed marriage.

To counter the risk, she says, couples must use the period of dating to collect enough data to try to prevent another devastating mistake. "In the early part of a relationship, you are setting the stage to *not* get your needs met if you can't make a direct request for the support you need, or talk about what you would like in a relationship—or if you can't say no to someone when you want to," says Hershenberg. "You can't learn if this is a person who will be a partner capable of giving you what you need, if you don't ask."

But, she adds, many people are afraid of being disappointed. "Ultimately, the fear is, 'If I ask for what I want, then I will be rejected or alone again.' Without putting that fear in check, people are walking around with blinders on."

If you don't establish what you need in a relationship and get married before your partner agrees to give it to you, your new marital status won't magically make your needs go away. A wedding ring won't grant mind-reading abilities to your new husband or wife, and a big reception won't help them support you emotionally in the years to come. You must make your expectations known before you move in together, or risk the turmoil of another divorce a few years hence.

"Marriage is not going to change anything—your or your partner's communication style or your insecurities—if you haven't dealt with these issues up front," Hershenberg says.

In short, don't be afraid to talk about your needs and expectations honestly. And if you are worried that honesty will jeopardize the new relationship, it's better to find out now. Indeed, Hershenberg advises changing a mindset of fear to one of boldness. To find a partner for a successful next marriage, make a commitment to yourself to act in your own best interest—and to explore whether the relationship will meet your needs before you leap.

"People are poised to make healthy relationship decisions if they can say to themselves, 'If the worst that can happen to me if I speak out for what I need is that this relationship ends, I can cope with that,'" Hershenberg explains. "After all, it's better to end a relationship if it won't give you the support you need, even if it's painful now, rather than have it continue and end eventually, with more heartache [and possibly another divorce]."

✤ Purge Destructive Patterns Before Trying Yet Again

Succeeding the second time around requires that you engage in serious self-examination. You must recognize and purge the patterns that doomed your prior relationship before heading out again.

The biggest issue could be your style of coping with stress. All marriages have significant stressors and problems—whether they survive or end up in divorce court. And, of course, there's no "perfect couple" cuddling, smiling and agreeing on everything in wedded bliss.

Everyone has spats and arguments, and tempers are bound to flare from time to time. This is true at the best of times, and it becomes still more critical when life gets tough.

Many couples look at a second marriage as a fresh start and a chance to achieve happiness with a new partner in a strong relationship.

~

Keith Sanford, Baylor University psychologist and neuroscience researcher, has spent years studying the differences between enduring and fractured unions. It turns out, he's found, that success and satisfaction may be related to the way couples work together during stressful times.

With his colleagues, Sanford has studied couples going through a variety of life stresses—including losing a job, the death of a parent or child, bankruptcy, or experiencing a chronic medical condition or even a trip to the emergency room.

The findings were stark: Spouses who accused their partner of causing the problem or complained that a partner's reaction was overblown, damaged the relationship. On the other hand, relationships were preserved when spouses refrained from fault-finding, criticism and other negative reactions.

This restraint is even more important than empathy, Sanford says. "When people face stressful life events, they are especially sensitive to negative behavior in their relationships, such as when a partner seems to be argumentative, overly emotional or withdrawn, or fails to do something that was expected. In contrast, they're less sensitive to positive behavior, such as giving each other comfort."

Because such issues likely contributed to the fissures that developed in a first marriage, it often behooves those making a second try to

A new marriage may involve children from prior relationships. Make sure that your blended family can work before forging ahead.

work hard on recognizing such patterns before embarking once again. By consciously changing both your coping and fighting styles, you can improve the odds that your next attempt at matrimony will last for the long haul. In fact, it's worth going to therapy to help you change your approach and awareness.

Hershenberg agrees: Contempt, blame and disrespect during times of stress can be fatal. But stonewalling a partner—withdrawing or refusing to respond when they try to communicate—is even worse, and it's one of the strongest predictors that a marriage will fail.

"When one person pursues talking about a problem and the other one shuts down completely and will not engage, it's one of the most corrosive patterns we see as marriage therapists," she notes.

♣ Leave Magical and Catastrophic Thinking Behind

For a second or third marriage to be healthy and supportive, you must face reality head-on. Don't buy into fantasies or delusions and try your level best to see the world as it is.

Your first goal should be working out your personal issues ahead of settling down. You need to give up the magical thinking that the relationship can make your problems disappear. Rather, it's important to seek out counseling or therapy so that demons from the past do not follow you into the new life you plan.

You should also be careful. If you think a not-so-great relationship must progress to matrimony or you will always be doomed to singlehood, reconsider. You deserve better, Hershenberg says.

"Oftentimes, the distinctive fear that a relationship might end is the result of what you think that means about your self-worth, your ability to be loved, your belief about what makes you a success or failure," she explains. Instead of settling, look toward a future in which you can

Blended-family issues, like rules, visitation and child support, need to be discussed before you get married.

find and sustain a healthier and happier marriage than you have experienced in the past. Take your time and break free of this urgent sense that you must preserve a relationship at all costs possible.

"I encourage both people in a relationship to find their voice and really communicate, to disclose their vulnerabilities and desires," she says. "How do you think about yourself as a couple? When you find the words and your behavior matches your real feelings and desires about what you need in a marriage, the confidence is empowering."

FIVE ISSUES YOU BOTH SHOULD DISCUSS BEFORE LEAPING AGAIN

1

HOME SWEET HOME IS WHERE?

If you have two homes, figure out together the best place—financially, logistically and emotionally—to set up house together. Does one home hold too many memories of an old, bad relationship or baggage from a previous marriage?

If one or both of you have children, consider their schools and neighborhoods and how much disruption a move may bring. It is critical to have space for all your children and to treat both partners' children equally. If kids aren't an issue for you, consider whether a fresh start in a new place would be best for you both.

THE CHILDREN

Yours, mine and ours. If either or both of you have children, there's more to figuring out a blended family than visitation schedules with the exes. Talk about existing rules and be clear on expectations about meals, bedtimes and discipline.

SEXUAL NEEDS

It's not romantic, but couples should talk frankly about sexual expectations, problems and needs before committing. Whether a man has erectile dysfunction or a woman finds sex painful, it is crucial to bring these issues into the open.

4

ELDERLY PARENTS

Baby boomers and Gen Xers may have older kids at home—but may also have elderly parents needing help. If either of you are part of a "sandwich" generation, be clear about how you plan to help, if needed, with each other's senior parents.

MONEY TALK

Do you need or want a prenup? Talk to your attorneys, financial advisers and each other to decide what's best. Don't forget to make any needed changes to your estate plans, wills and other financial agreements.

Words of Love

POETS, PUNDITS AND PHILOSOPHERS ALIKE SHARE THEIR
THOUGHTS ON LIFE'S MOST POWERFUL AND LASTING FEELING.

♥

"All is fair in love and war."

*Francis Edward Smedley,
in* Frank Fairleigh

"'Tis better to have loved and lost than never to have loved at all."

*Alfred,
Lord Tennyson*

"Love is an endless act of forgiveness."

Beyoncé

"The greatest thing you'll ever learn is just to love and be loved in return."

Eden Ahbez

"The course of true love never did run smooth."

Shakespeare, in
A Midsummer Night's Dream

"At the touch of love, everyone becomes a poet."

Plato

"Gravitation cannot be held responsible for [falling in love]."

Albert Einstein

"The smile is
the beginning
of love."
Mother Teresa

"We rise and fall
and light from
dying embers,
remembrances that
hope and love last
longer. And love is
love is love is love is
love is love is love is
love cannot be killed
or swept aside."
Lin-Manuel Miranda

"If nothing
saves us from
death, at
least love
should save
us from life."
Pablo Neruda

"Love is
something sent
from heaven
to worry the
hell out of you."
Dolly Parton

"Love loves
to love love."
James Joyce

A

Affairs, extramarital, 16, 58, 64
Afterglow, 22, 124
Arguments. *See* Conflict, marital
Attachment theory, 42, 47
Autonomy, 40–44, 112

B

Blended family, 135–137

C

Cancer, 73–76
Cardiovascular disease, 68–70
Casual touch, 109
Catastrophic thinking, 136–137
Character. *See* Personality
Chemical attraction, 22
Children
 leaving home, rebuilding
  marriage after, 96–103
 before marriage, 17
 parenting challenges,
  80–85
 remarriage and, 135–137
Choice, of partner, 12, 16, 27, 31,
 43–44
Clitoral stimulation, 124, 125
Closeness
 emotional, 22, 47, 54
 physical, 59, 109

Communication
 couple satisfaction and, 25,
  31–32, 34
 marital conflict and, 85–89,
  113
 remarriage and, 136–137
Compatibility, 25, 32
Compromise, 47, 89
Conflict, marital
 advice on, 32, 35
 how to handle, 31, 86–89
 stress and, 134–135
Connectedness, 40–44, 112
Contempt, 16, 25, 135
Cortisol levels, 76
Couples
 famous (historical),
  13–16, 19
 parenthood and, 80–85
 satisfaction factors, 25
 as a team, 35–36

D

Dating, 22–23
 online, 24
 before remarriage, 133
Defensiveness, 25, 35
Desire(s)
 dip in, 109, 110
 expressing, 108, 111, 138
 female orgasm and, 125

research of, 121–122
 stimulating, 117
Destructive behaviors/patterns,
 134–136
Differentiation, marital
 attachment and, 42–47, 53
Disagreements. *See* Conflict,
 marital
Divorce
 after remarriage, 131,
  133–134
 behavior predicting, 25–26,
  35
 remarriage after.
  See Remarriage
Divorce rate, 31, 80
 remarriage and, 131, 133
Dopamine, 22, 109, 116, 124,
 125, 127

E

Elderly parents, remarriage and,
 137
Empathy, 32–34, 36, 103, 135
Empty nest, 96–103
Entrainment, 124
Erectile dysfunction (ED), 44,
 110, 137
Extramarital affairs, 16, 58, 64

F

Finances, remarriage and, 130, 137
Financial stability, 21
First kiss, 22, 127
Flexibility, 89
Fresh start, remarriage as, 134–136

G

Gender ID/Gender roles, 17, 57
Gridlock, marital, 50–53

H

Health benefits
  of committed love, 66–77
  of regular sex, 116
Heart attack, 68–73
Humor, sense of, 35–36

I

In-law relationships, 90–95
Infidelity, marital, 16, 58, 64
Interdependence, 47
Intimacy, 44
  maintaining, 116, 117
  other-validated, 49
  self-validated, 49–50
"Intimacy-desire paradox," 109

J

Jealousy, 62, 93

K

Kissing, 22, 126–127

L

Life transitions
  coping with stress in, 134–136
  rebuilding marriage after children leave home, 96–103
Love
  committed. *See* Marriage
  finding, key elements in, 20–27
  flourish in, profundity and, 63
  new vs. old, 56, 59
  passionate vs. romantic, 54–65
  quotations on, 138–139
Love match. *See* Soul mate

M

Magical thinking, 136–137
Major histocompatibility complex (MHC), 22
Manipulation, 48–49
Marriage
  age at, 12, 17, 18
  conflict in, navigating, 86–89
  happiest, science of, 28–37
  health benefits of, 66–77
  history of, 10–19
  in-law relationships and, 90–95
  lengthy, advice on, 31, 32, 35, 64
  rebuilding after children leave home, 96–103
  second. *See* Remarriage
  successful, relationship skills for, 40–53
Marriage rates,
  U.S. vs. European, 18
Masturbation, 115, 116
Mental health, 21, 26
Millennials, marriage and, 17
Mind games, 48

N

Needs, communicating before remarriage, 133–134, 137
Neurochemicals, 22. *See also* Dopamine; Oxytocin

O

Online dating, 24
Open love, 62
Orgasm, 116, 118–125
Oxytocin, 116, 124, 125, 127

Index

P

Parenthood, challenges of, 80–85

Parents

    elderly, remarriage and, 137

    in-law relationships and, 90–95

Passion/Passionate love, 44–45, 47, 54–65

Patience, 16, 35–36

Personality, 20, 22, 25, 32

Physical appearance, 23, 25, 113

Polyamory, 58, 63

Premarital sex, 16

Prenuptial agreement, 137

Profundity, romantic, 59–61, 63

R

Red flag behavior, 25–26, 35

Relationships

    differences in, 31–33, 129–131

    egalitarianism in, 110

    flourishing in, 55, 62–64, 64

    lengthy, consistencies in, 36

    similarities in, 23, 25

    skills for successful marriage, 40–53

    in stressful situations, 134–136

    supportive. *See* Supportive relationships

Remarriage, 128–137

Reproduction, 122

Resilience, 53

Respect, 31, 34, 36, 49

Responsibility

    for own happiness, 32, 45

    shared. *See* Shared responsibility

Romantic love/profundity, 20, 42, 43, 54–65

S

Sadism, mutual, 48–49

Same-sex marriage, 17, 57

Self-examination, remarriage and, 134–136

Serotonin, 127

Setting up home

    after remarriage, 137

    without marriage, 129–131

Sex

    anxiety and, 44

    eyes-open, 45, 47

    frequency of, 56, 110

    orgasm and, 118–125

    physiological barriers to, 110, 114

    premarital, 26

    regular, health benefits of, 116

Sex life, in committed relationship

    changes in, 106

    tips on maintaining, 107–117

Sexual arousal, female, 125

Sexual needs, 108, 137

Shared responsibility, 12

    marital success and, 18

    parenting and, 84

Smooching, 22, 126–127

Soul mate, 15, 20, 24

Stonewalling, 26, 135

Stress/Stressors, 76, 134–135

Supportive relationships, 25–26

    health issues and, 66–77

T

Tension

    effect on children, 80

    in-law relationships and, 90–95

Testosterone, 110

Tolerance, 36

Touching, 44–45, 109

Z

Zero Negativity Challenge, 84

PHOTO CREDITS

COVER From top: Katsumi Murouchi/Getty Images. Yulia Naumenko/Getty Images **2–3** pixdeluxe/Getty Images **4–5** SolStock/Getty Images **6–7** PeopleImages/Getty Images **8–9** pixdeluxe/Getty Images **10–11** Camerique/Getty Images **12–13** UniversalImagesGroup/Getty Images **14–15** Print Collector/Getty Images **16–17** From left: Heritage Images/Getty Images. Imagno/Getty Images **18–19** Fotosearch/Getty Images **20–21** Ja_inter/Getty Images **22–23** EstherQueen999/Shutterstock **24–25** Siberian Art/Shutterstock **26–27** mathisworks/Getty Images **28–29** Westend61/Getty Images **30–31** Westend61/Getty Images **32–33** From left: bortonia/Getty Images. Westend61/Getty Images **34–35** Westend61/Getty Images **36–37** Westend61/Getty Images **38–39** Flashpop/Getty Images **40–41** SolStock/Getty Images **42–43** SolStock/Getty Images **44–45** SolStock/Getty Images **46–47** SolStock/Getty Images **48–49** SolStock/Getty Images **50–51** SolStock/Getty Images **52–53** SolStock/Getty Images **54–55** andriikobryn/Getty Images **56–57** fizkes/Shutterstock/Getty Images **58–59** PeopleImages/Getty Images **60–61** Kathrin Ziegler/Getty Images **62–63** digitalskillet/Getty Images **64–65** Thomas Barwick/Getty Images **66–67** Klaus Vedfelt/Getty Images **68–69** Klaus Vedfelt/Getty Images **70–71** Klaus Vedfelt/Getty Images **72–73** Klaus Vedfelt/Getty Images **74–75** Klaus Vedfelt/Getty Images **76–77** From left: Atiketta Sangasaeng/Shutterstock. Science Photo Library/Getty Images. Natalie Prinz/EyeEm/Getty Images. JoKMedia/Getty Images **78–79** Westend61/Getty Images **80–81** Westend61/Getty Images **82–83** Westend61/Getty Images **84–85** Westend61/Getty Images **86–87** dane_mark/Getty Images **88–89** dane_mark/Getty Images **90–91** skynesher/Getty Images **92–93** skynesher/Getty Images **94–95** skynesher/Getty Images **96–97** Kelvin Murray/Getty Images **98–99** Kelvin Murray/Getty Images **100–101** Kelvin Murray/Getty Images **102–103** NC **104–105** Sporrer/Rupp/Getty Images **106–107** From left: CreativaImages/Getty Images. bortonia/Getty Images **108–109** Steve Prezant/Getty Images **110–111** People Images/Getty Images **112–113** Jon Feingersh Photography Inc/Getty Images **114–115** Cavan Images/Getty Images **116–117** bortonia/Getty Images **118–119** PeopleImages/Getty Images **120–121** Jonathan Storey/Getty Images **122–123** Jonathan Storey/Getty Images **124–125** NC **126–127** Laetizia Haessig / EyeEm **128–129** James Henry/Getty Images **130–131** RomanR/Shutterstock **132–133** ViewFinder nilsophon/Shutterstock **134–135** James Henry/Getty Images **136–137** Altrendo Images/Shutterstock **138–139** zf L/Getty Images **SPINE** Morrison1977/Getty Images **BACK COVER** Flashpop/Getty Images

SPECIAL THANKS TO CONTRIBUTING WRITERS

Carrie Arnold, Sherry Baker, Temma Ehrenfeld, Mark Hay, Anne Lane, Shira Rubin, Davia Sills, Jason Teich, Lauren Weltbank, Emily Willingham

CENTENNIAL BOOKS

An Imprint of
Centennial Media, LLC
40 Worth St., 10th Floor
New York, NY 10013, U.S.A.

CENTENNIAL BOOKS is a trademark of Centennial Media, LLC

All rights reserved. No part of this publication may be reproduced, stored in a retrieval system,
or transmitted in any form or by any means (including electronic, mechanical, photocopying, recording,
or otherwise) without prior written permission from the publisher.

ISBN 978-1-951274-36-8

Distributed by
Simon & Schuster, Inc.
1230 Avenue of the Americas
New York, NY 10020, U.S.A.

For information about custom editions, special sales and premium and corporate purchases,
please contact Centennial Media at contact@centennialmedia.com.

Manufactured in China

© 2020 by Centennial Media, LLC

10 9 8 7 6 5 4 3 2 1

Publishers & Co-Founders Ben Harris, Sebastian Raatz
Editorial Director Annabel Vered
Creative Director Jessica Power
Executive Editor Janet Giovanelli
Deputy Editors Ron Kelly, Alyssa Shaffer
Design Director Martin Elfers
Art Directors Runyon Hall, Natali Suasnavas, Joseph Ulatowski
Copy/Production Patty Carroll, Angela Taormina
Assistant Art Director Jaclyn Loney
Photo Editor April O'Neil
Production Manager Paul Rodina
Production Assistant Alyssa Swiderski
Editorial Assistant Tiana Schippa
Sales & Marketing Jeremy Nurnberg